Susie's Whimsical Halloween
Coloring Book for all ages

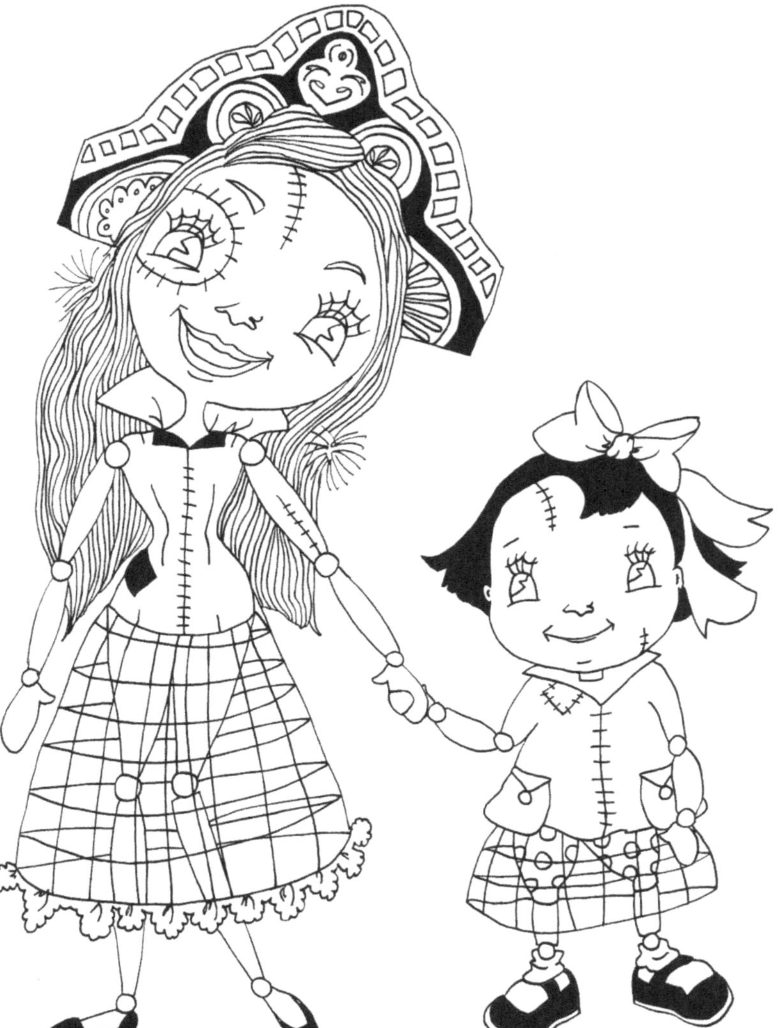

Illustrated by Susie Scott

www.susiescott.com
www.facebook.com/susiescottshop

Susie Scott • Hope, ID
www.susiescott.com • ©2017

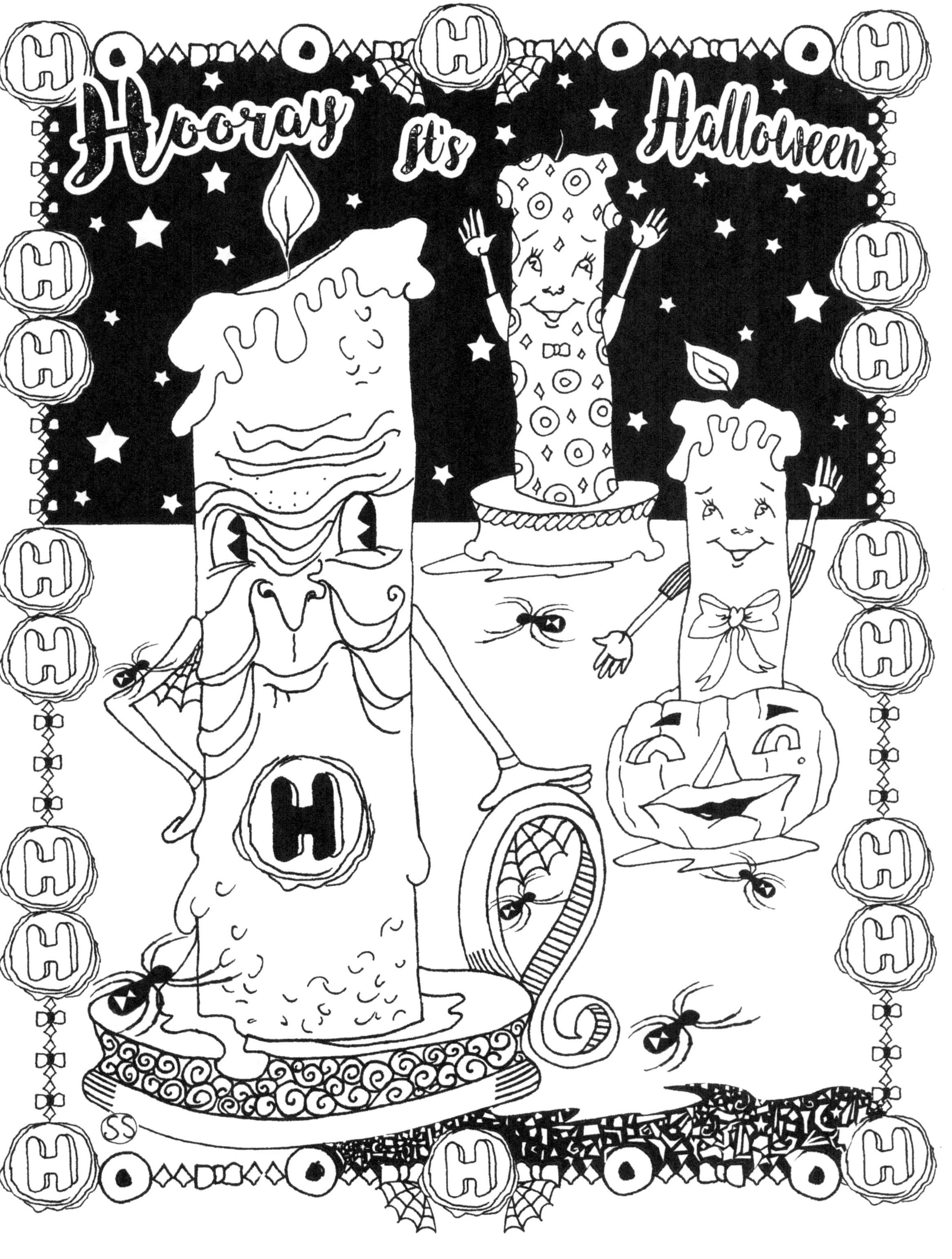
Hooray It's Halloween
SS

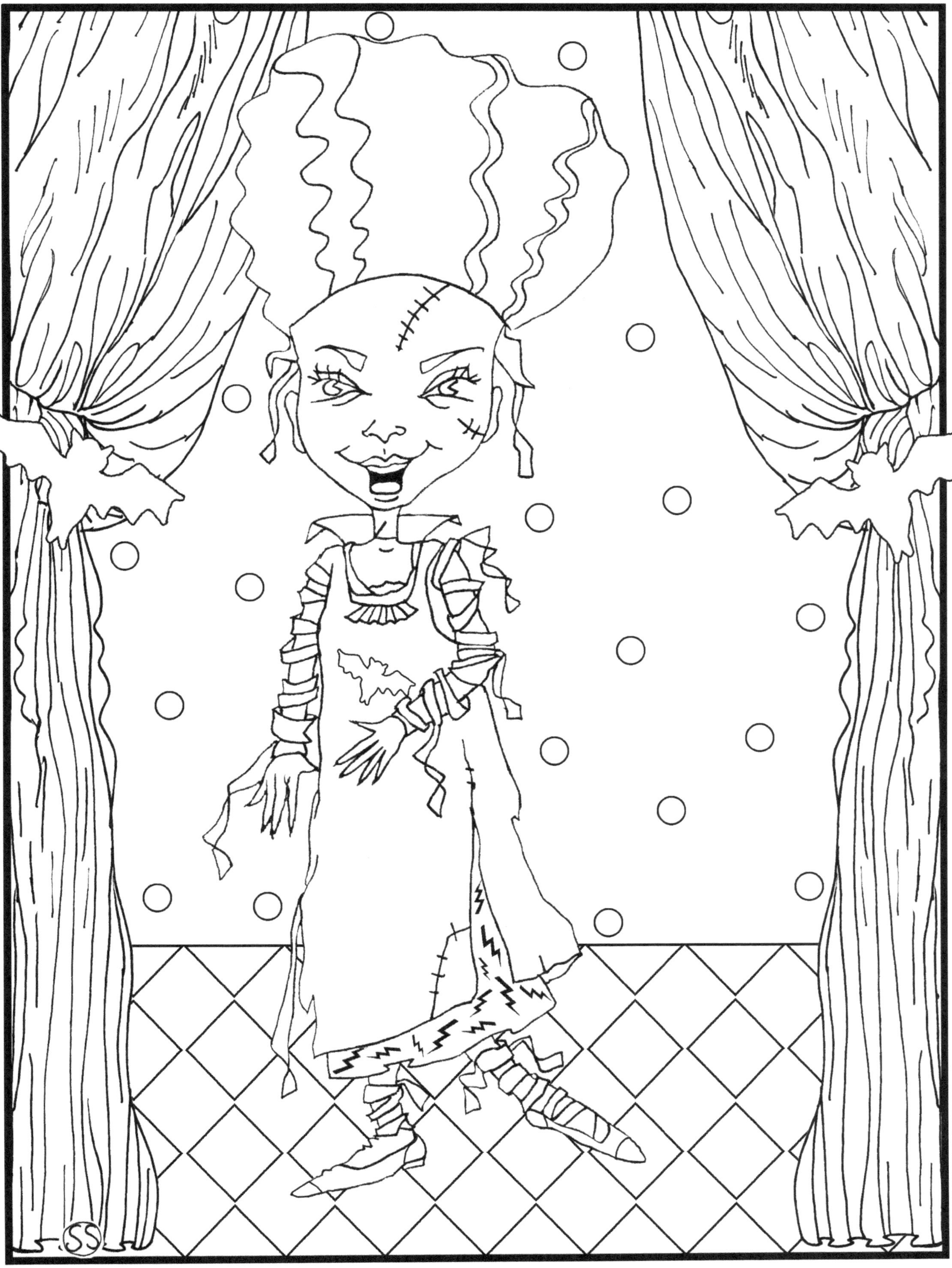
SS

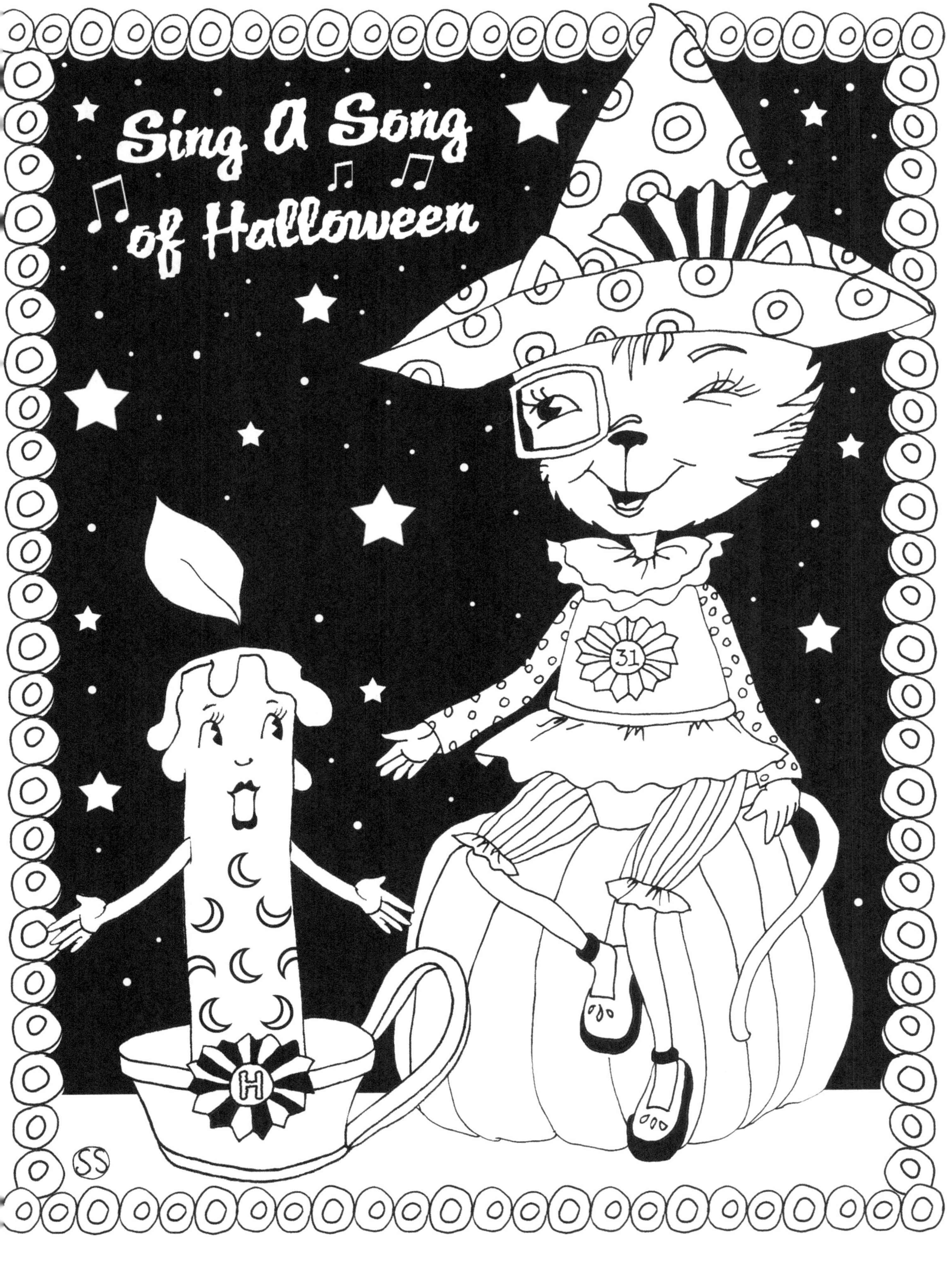
Sing A Song
of Halloween
31
H
SS

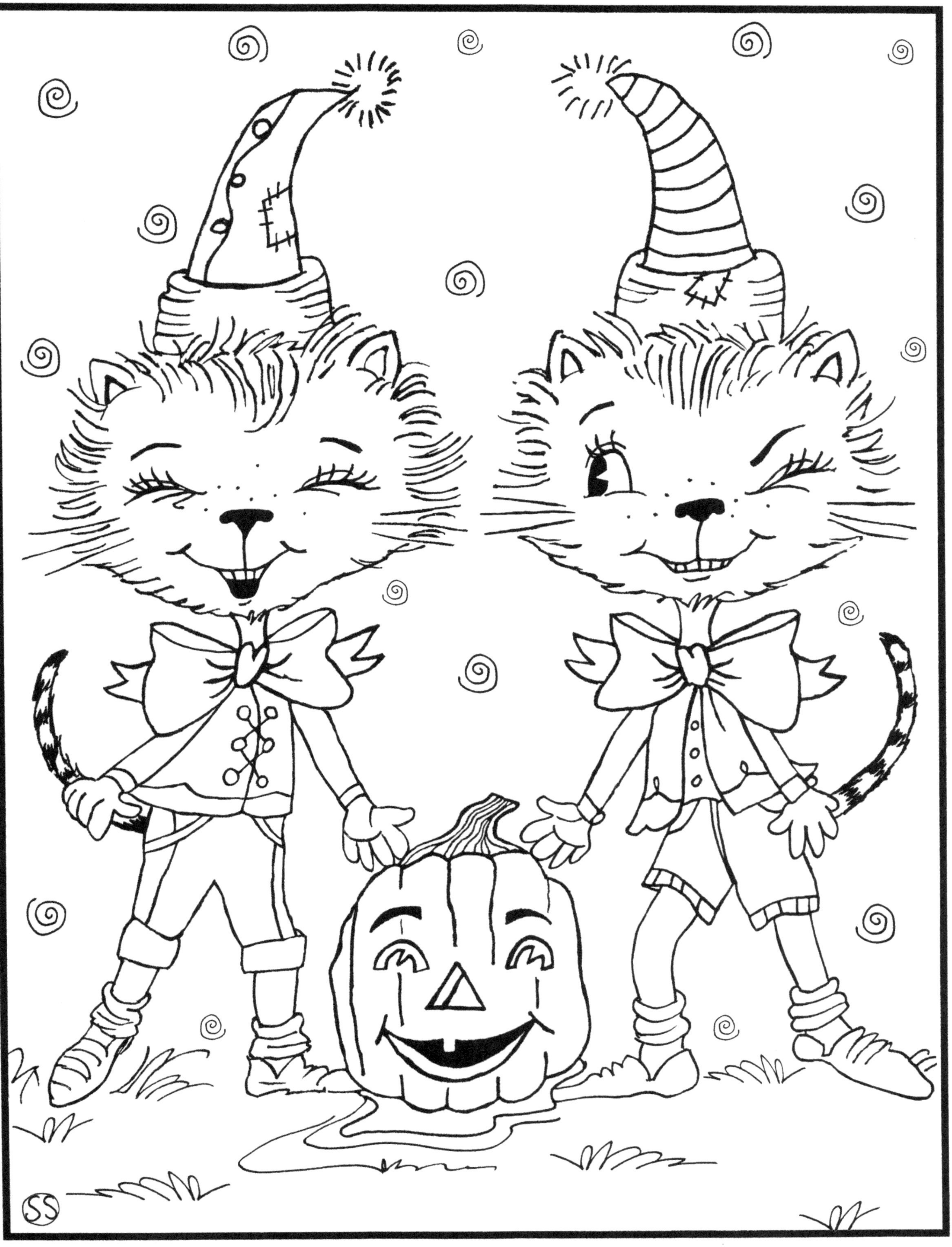
SS

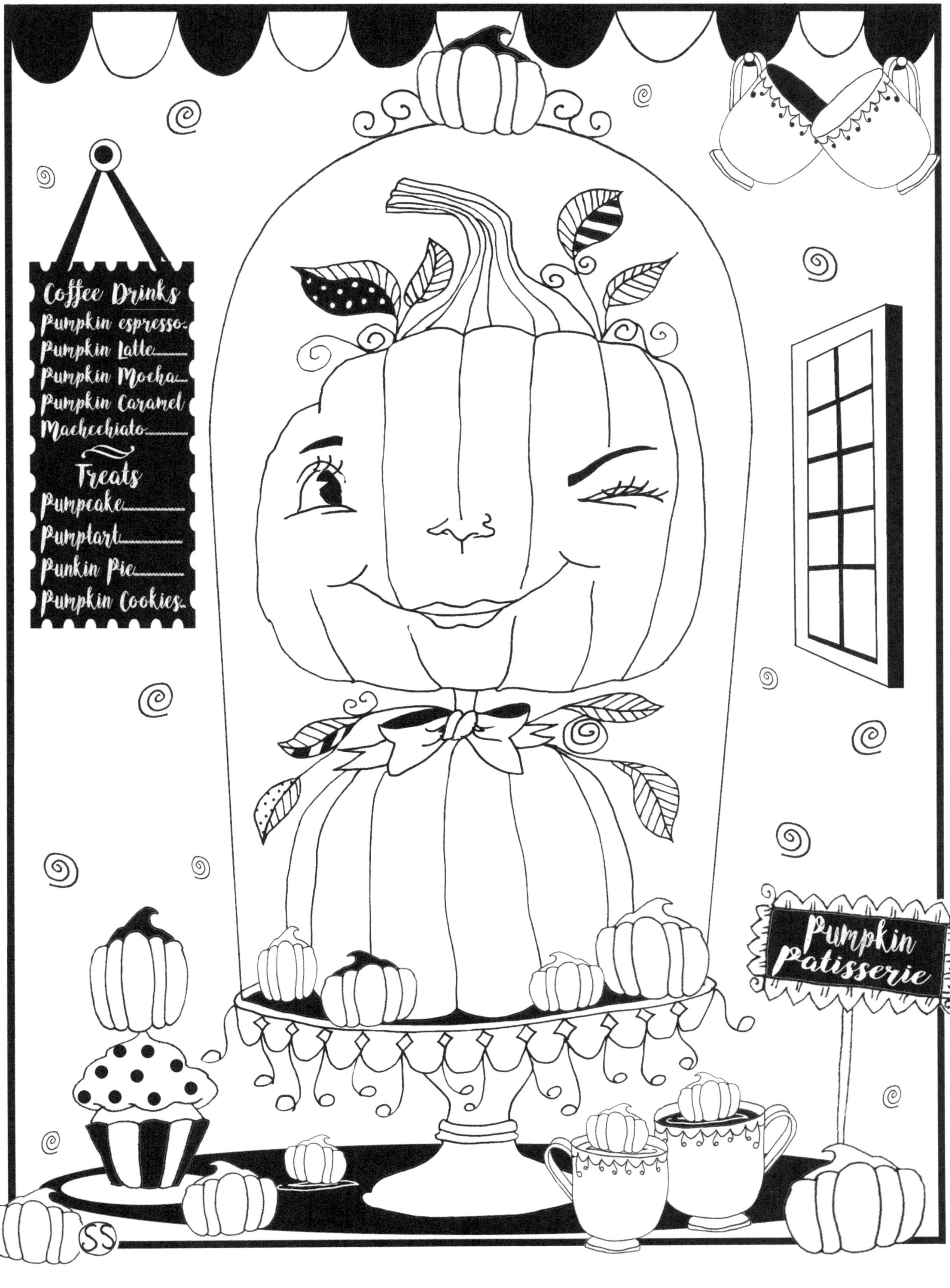

Coffee Drinks
Pumpkin espresso
Pumpkin Latte
Pumpkin Mocha
Pumpkin Caramel
Machcchiato
Treats
Pumpcake
Pumptart
Punkin Pie
Pumpkin Cookies
Pumpkin Patisserie
SS

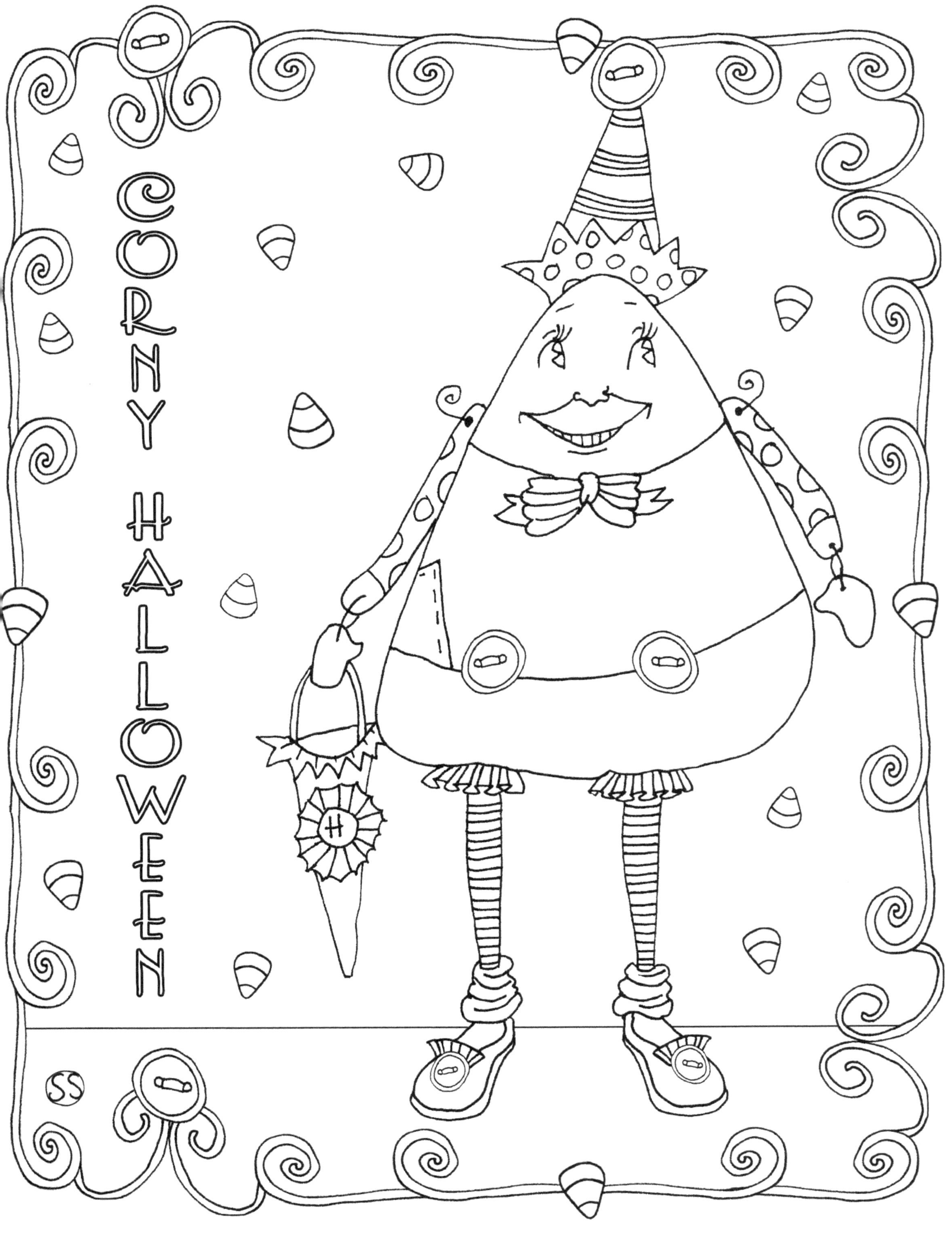
CORNY HALLOWEEN
H
SS

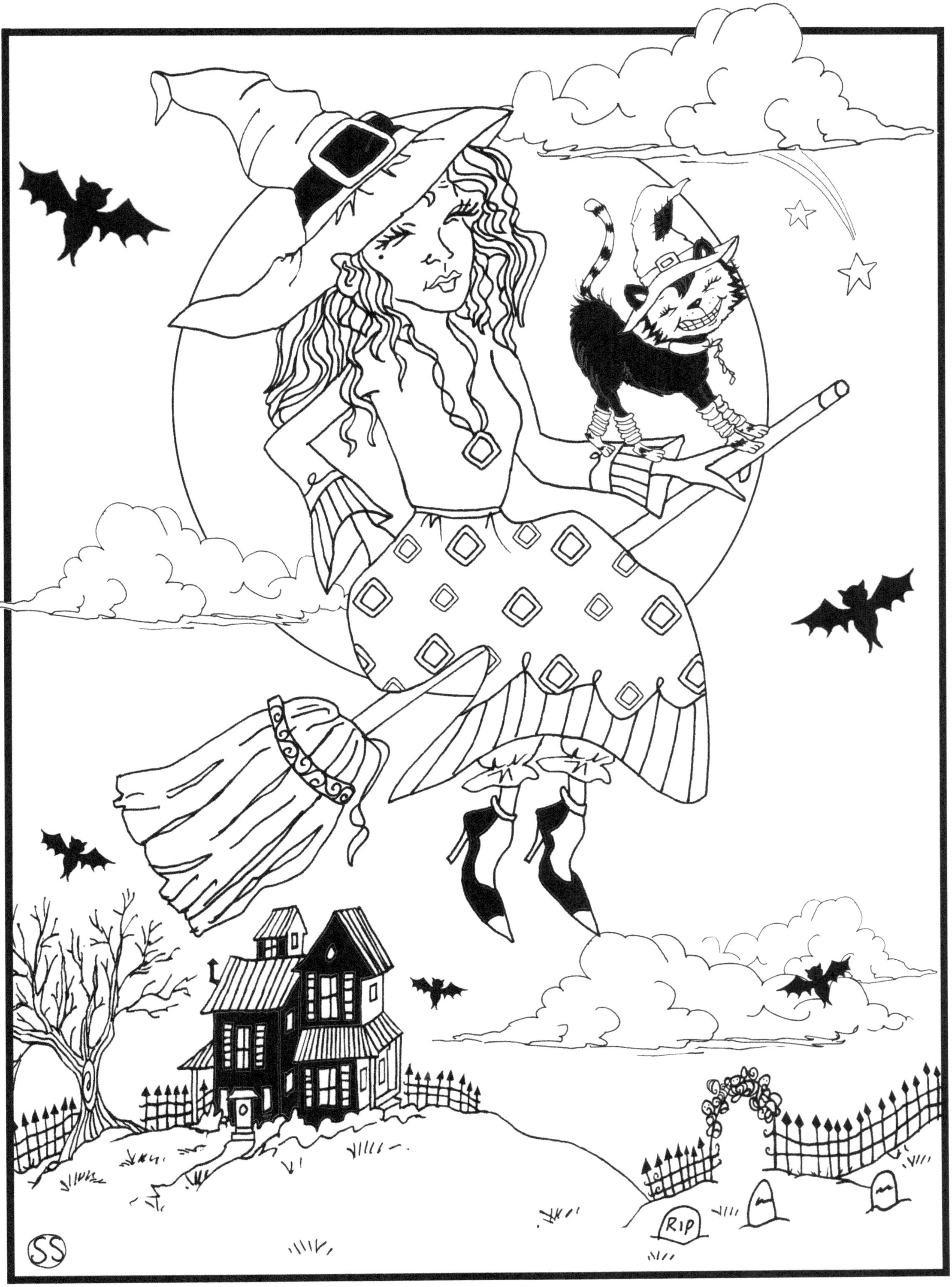
Rip

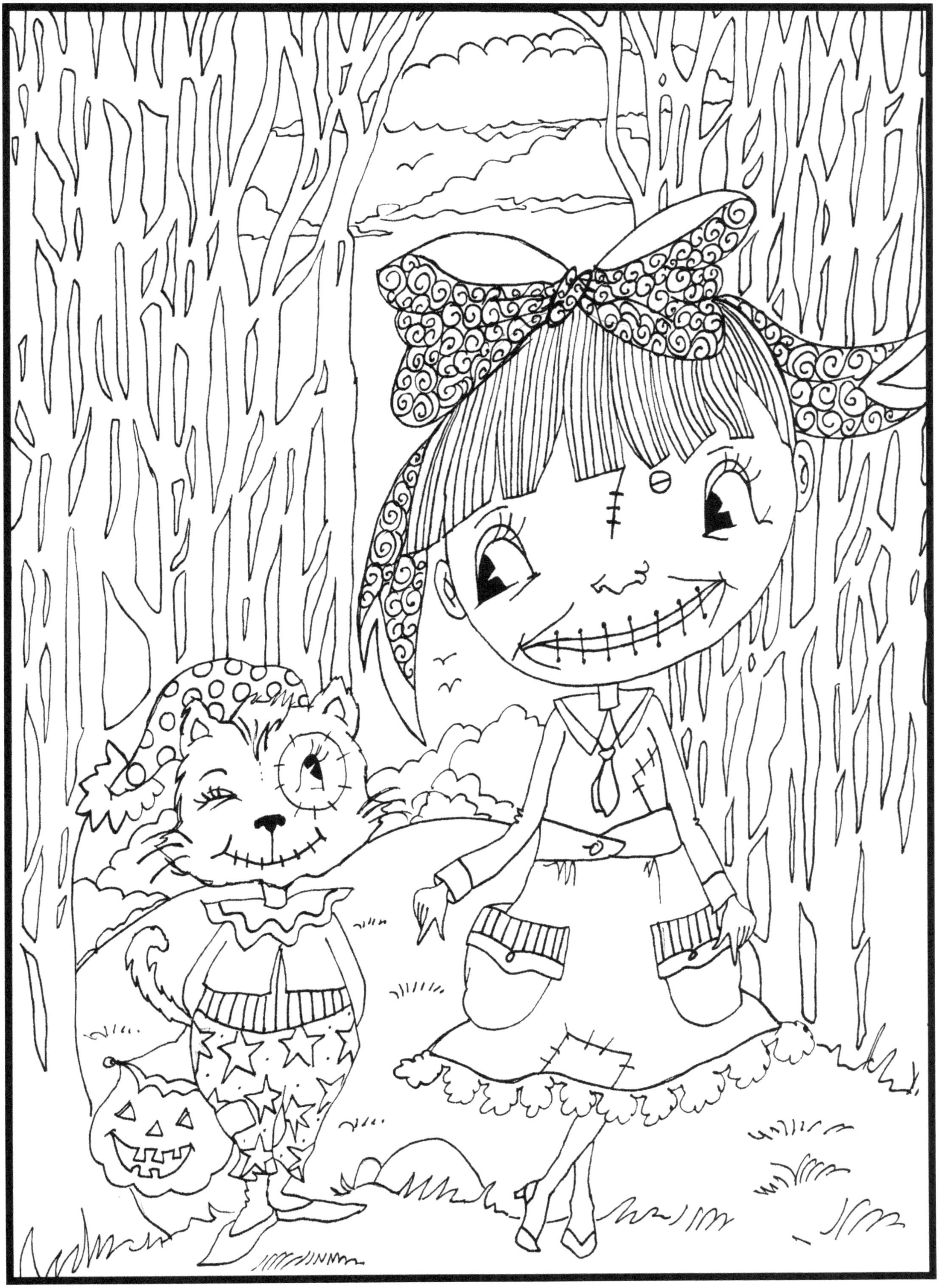

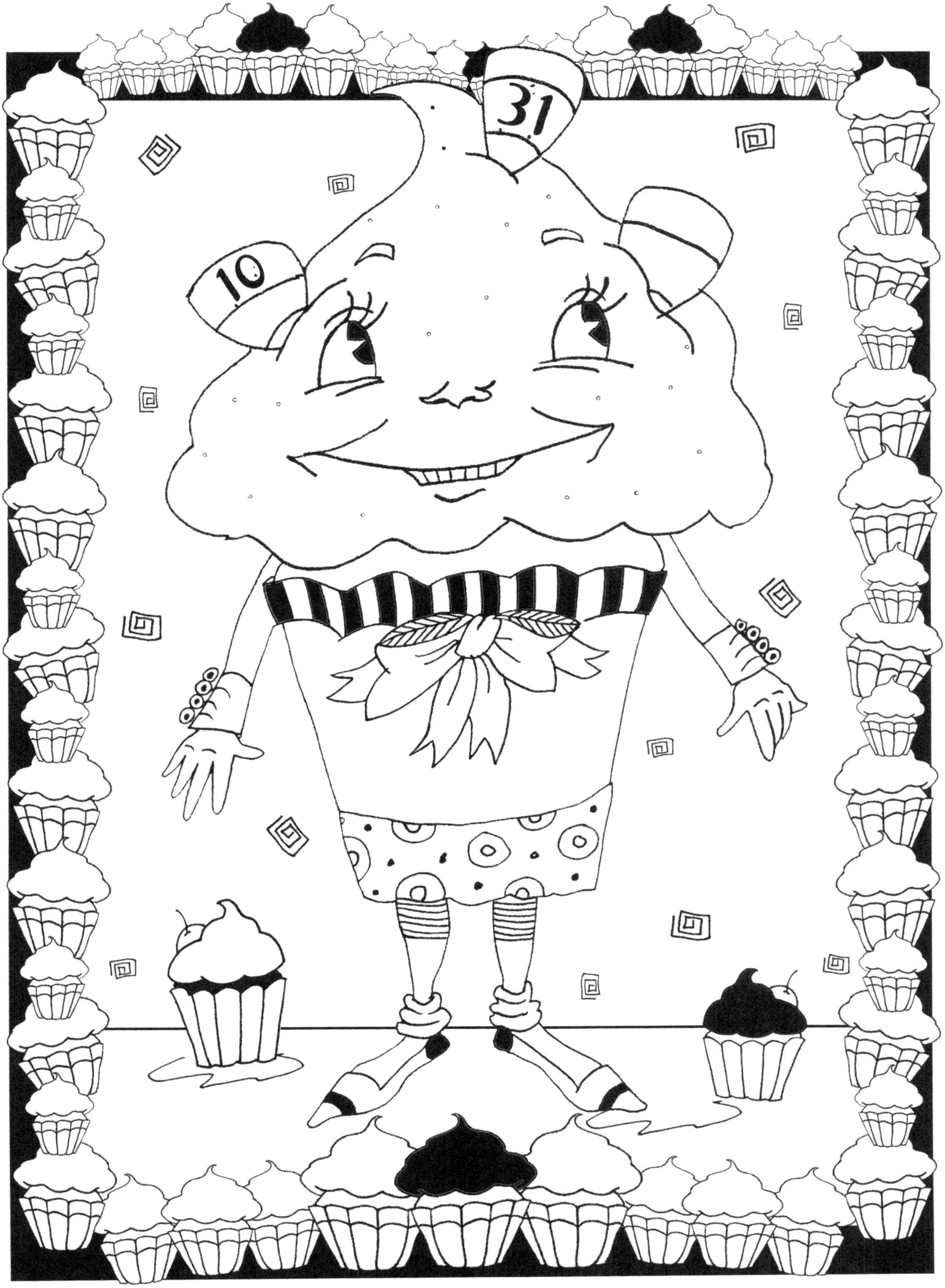
10
31

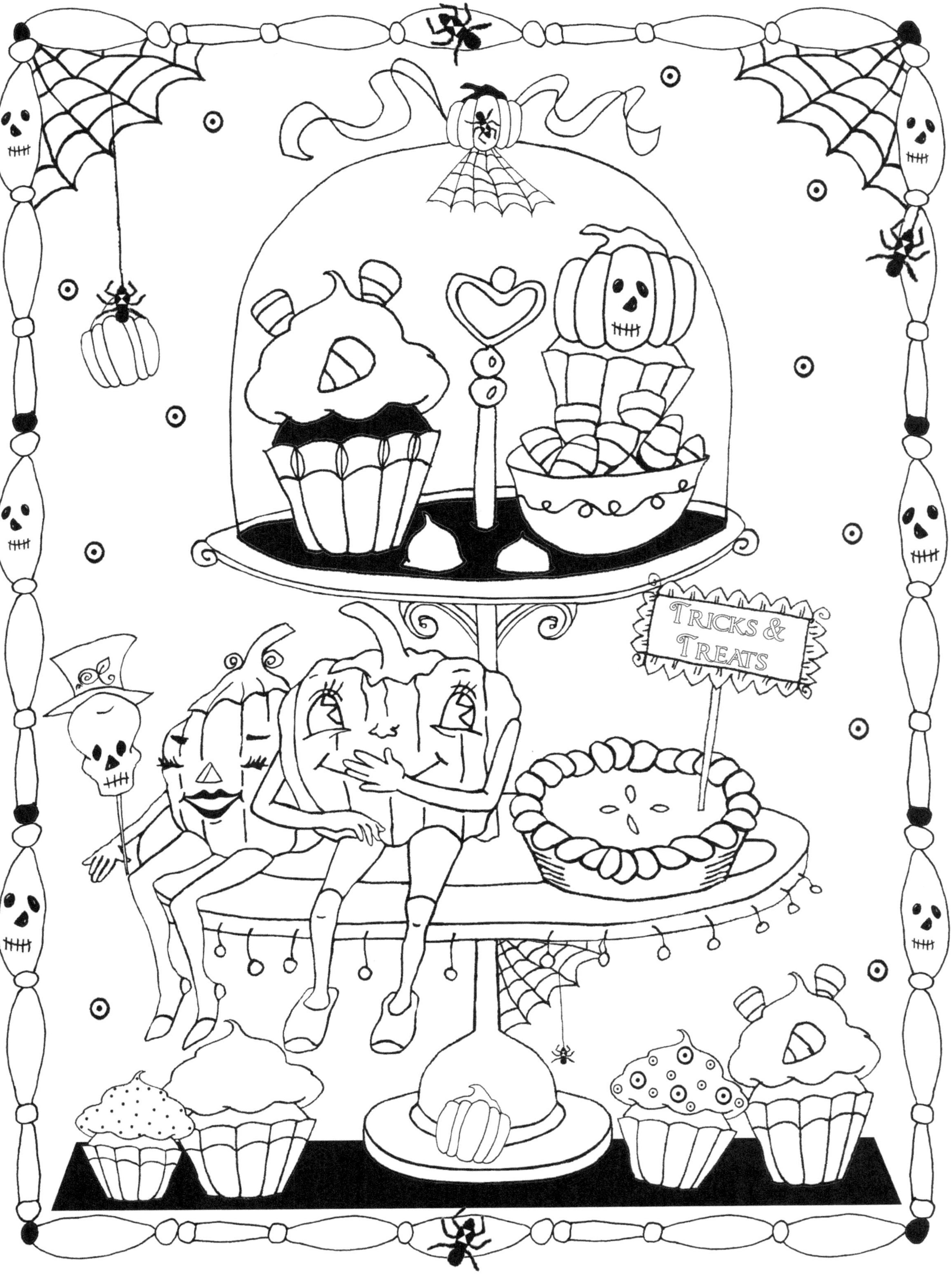
Tricks &
Treats

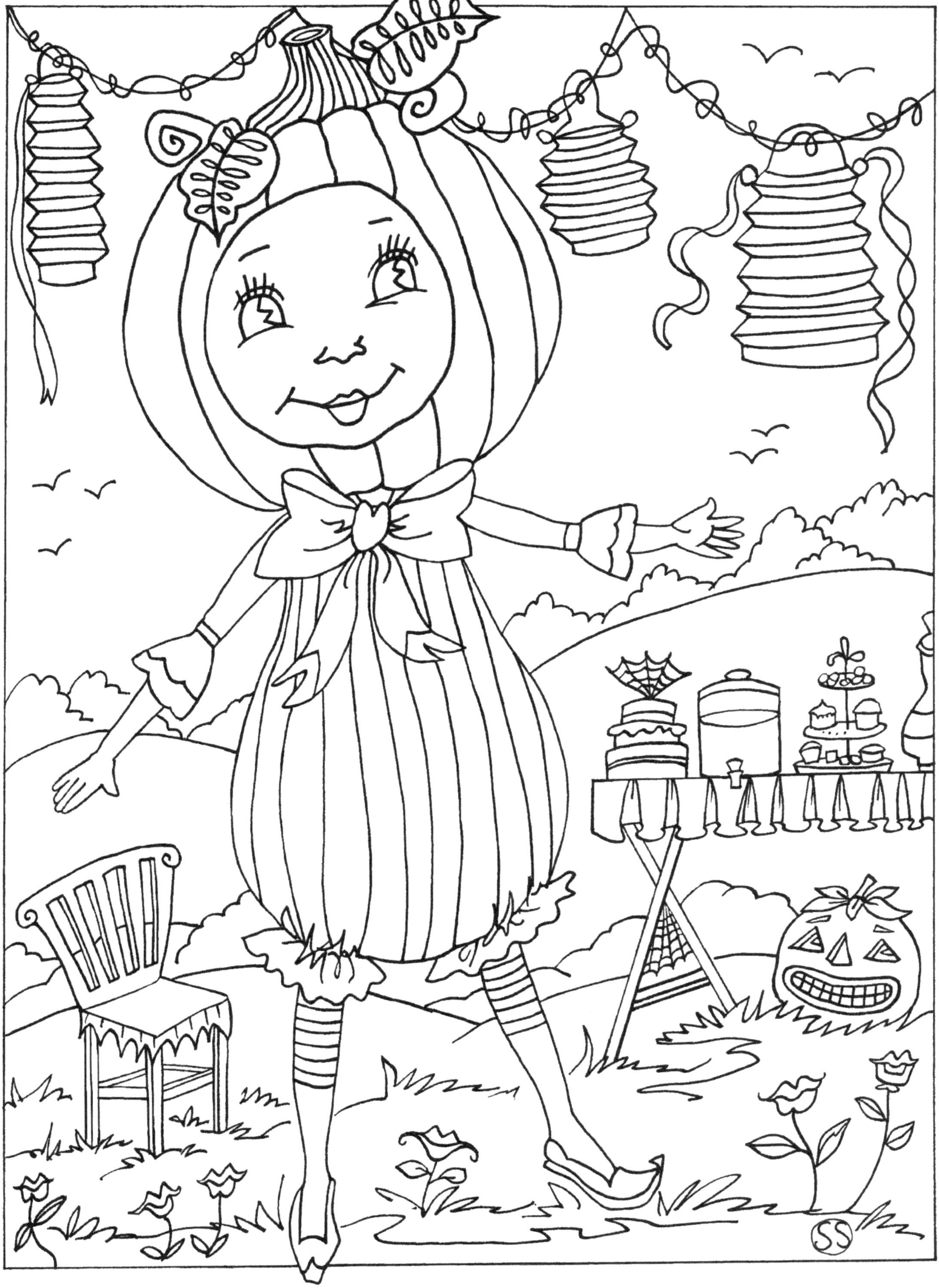
SS

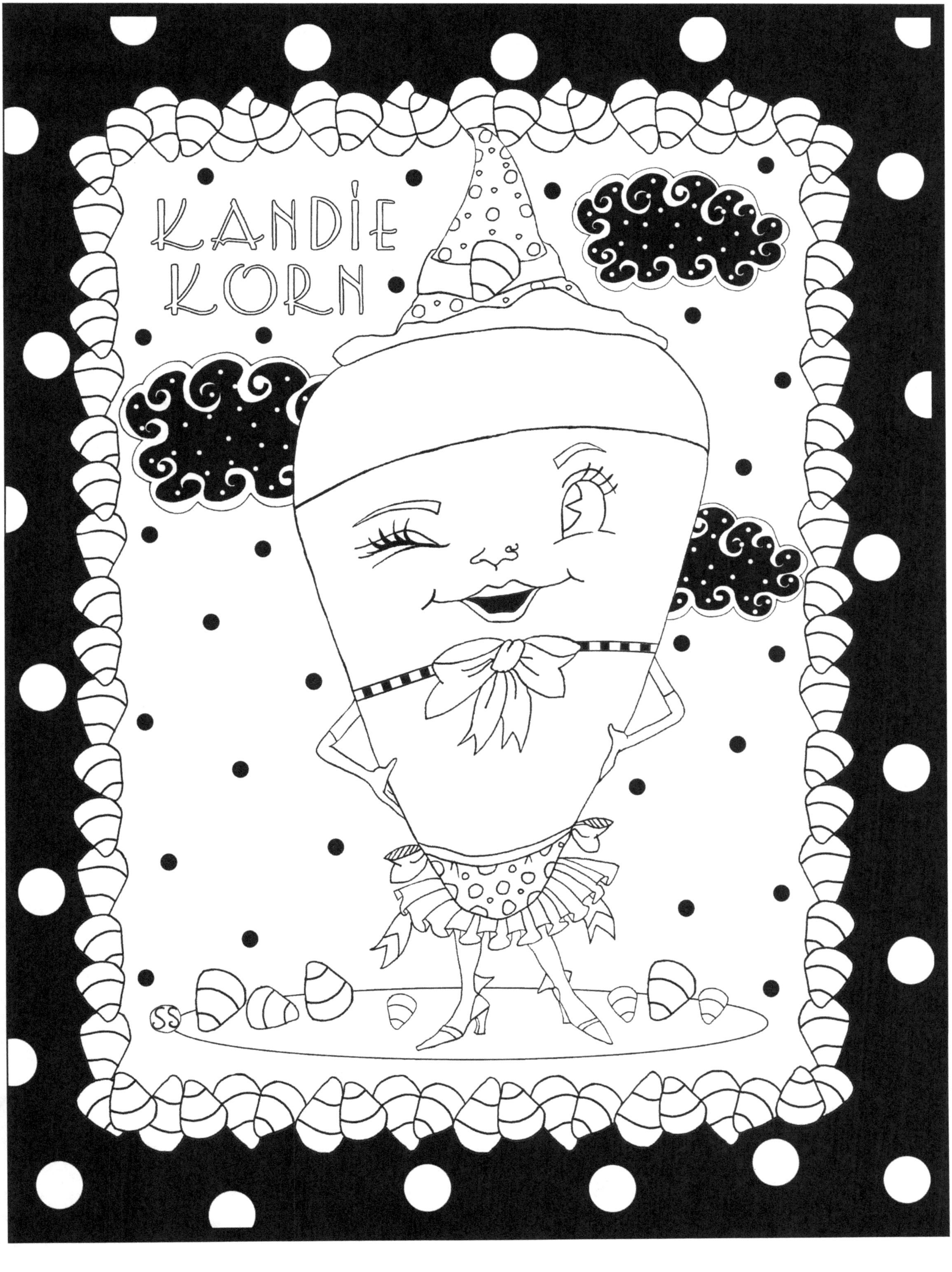
KANDIE
KORN
SS

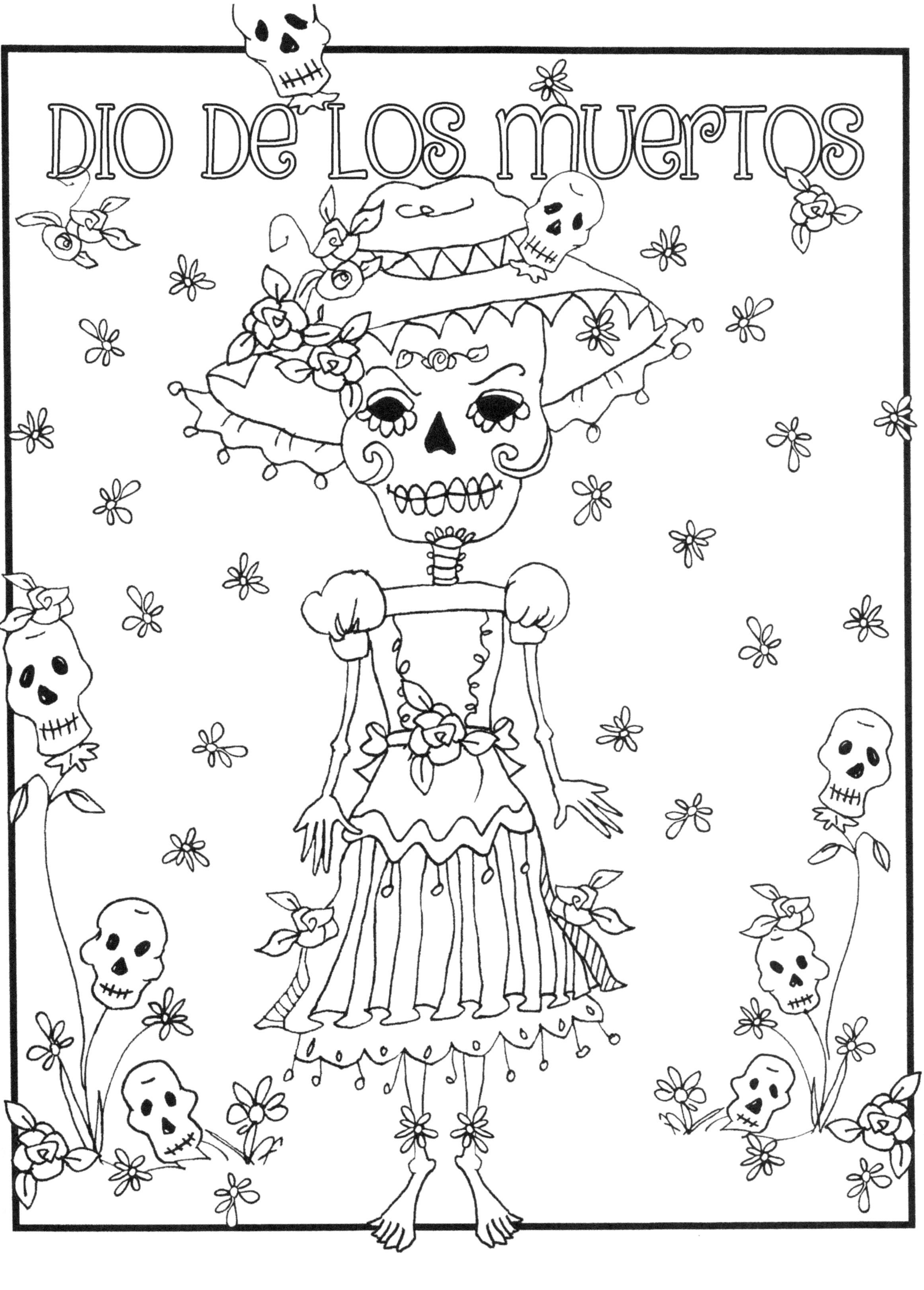
DIO DE LOS MUERTOS

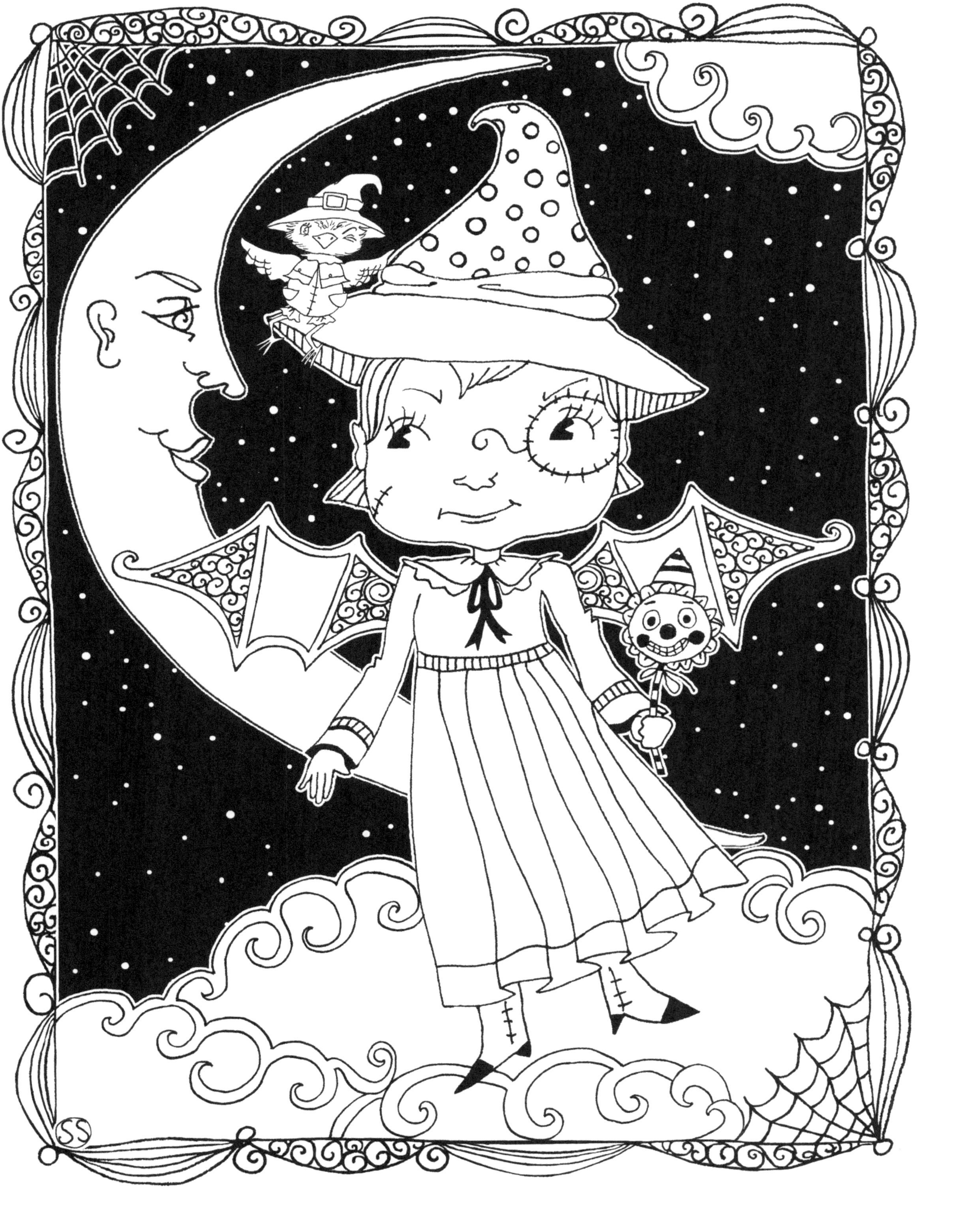
SS

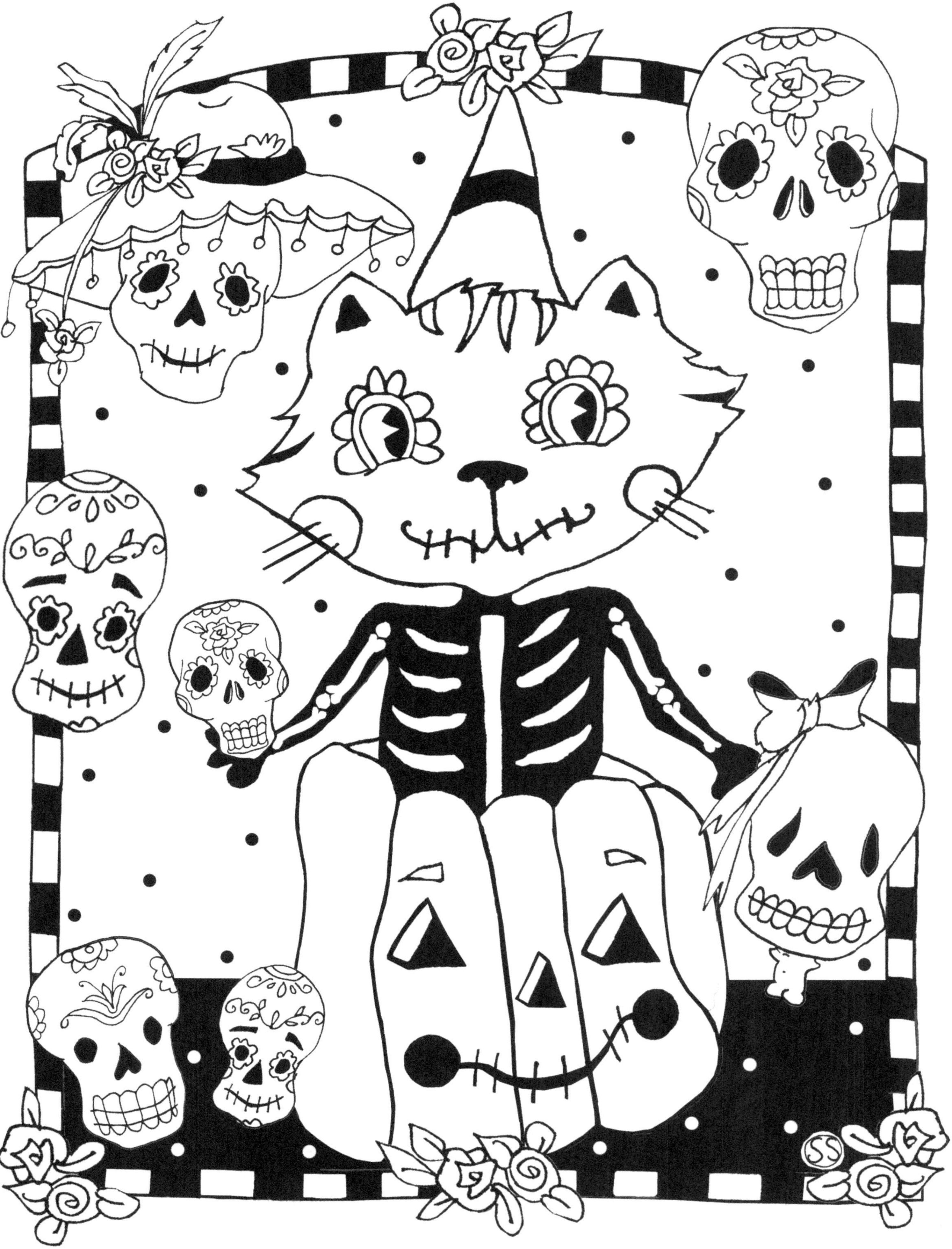

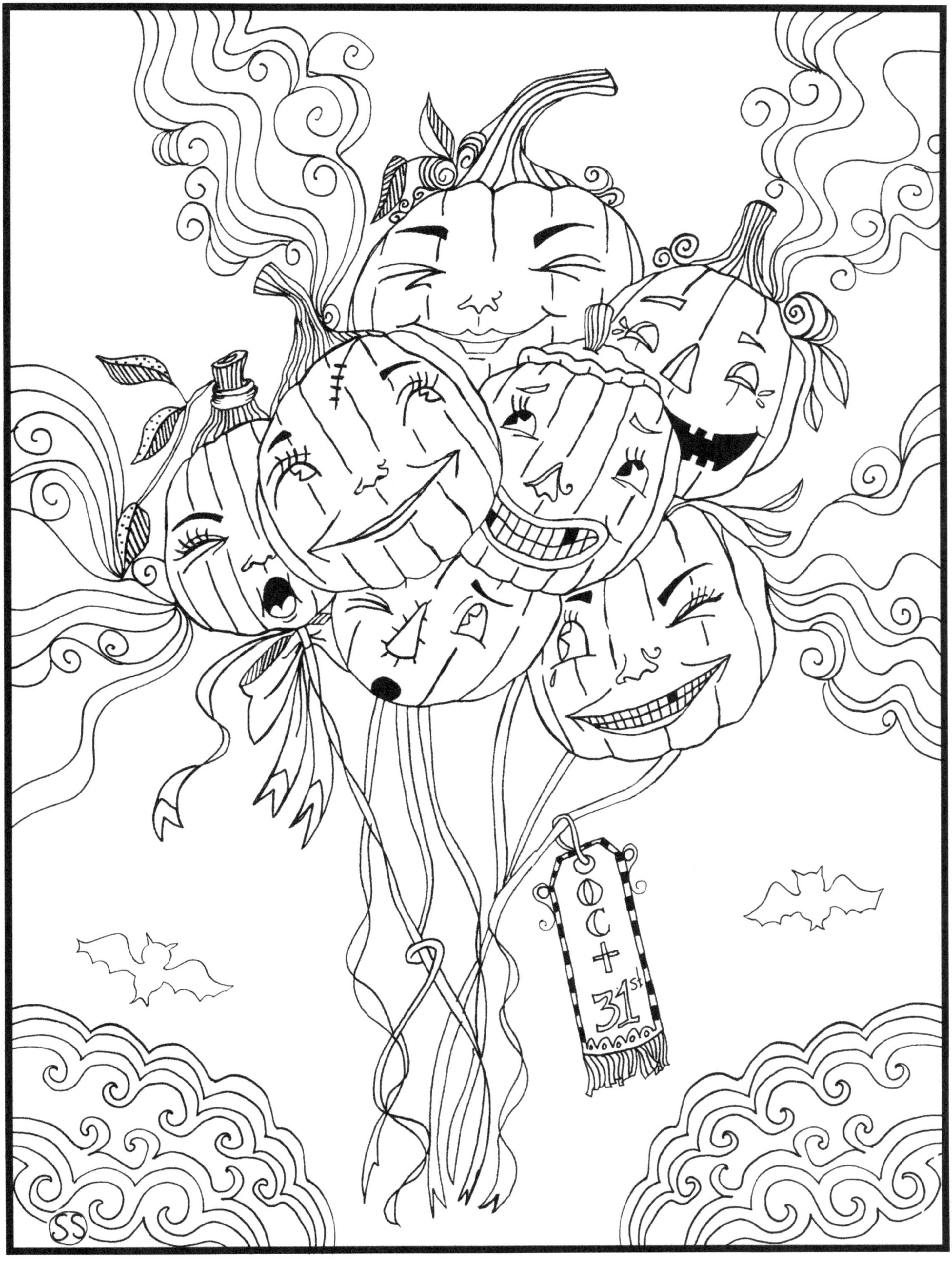
Oct
31st
SS

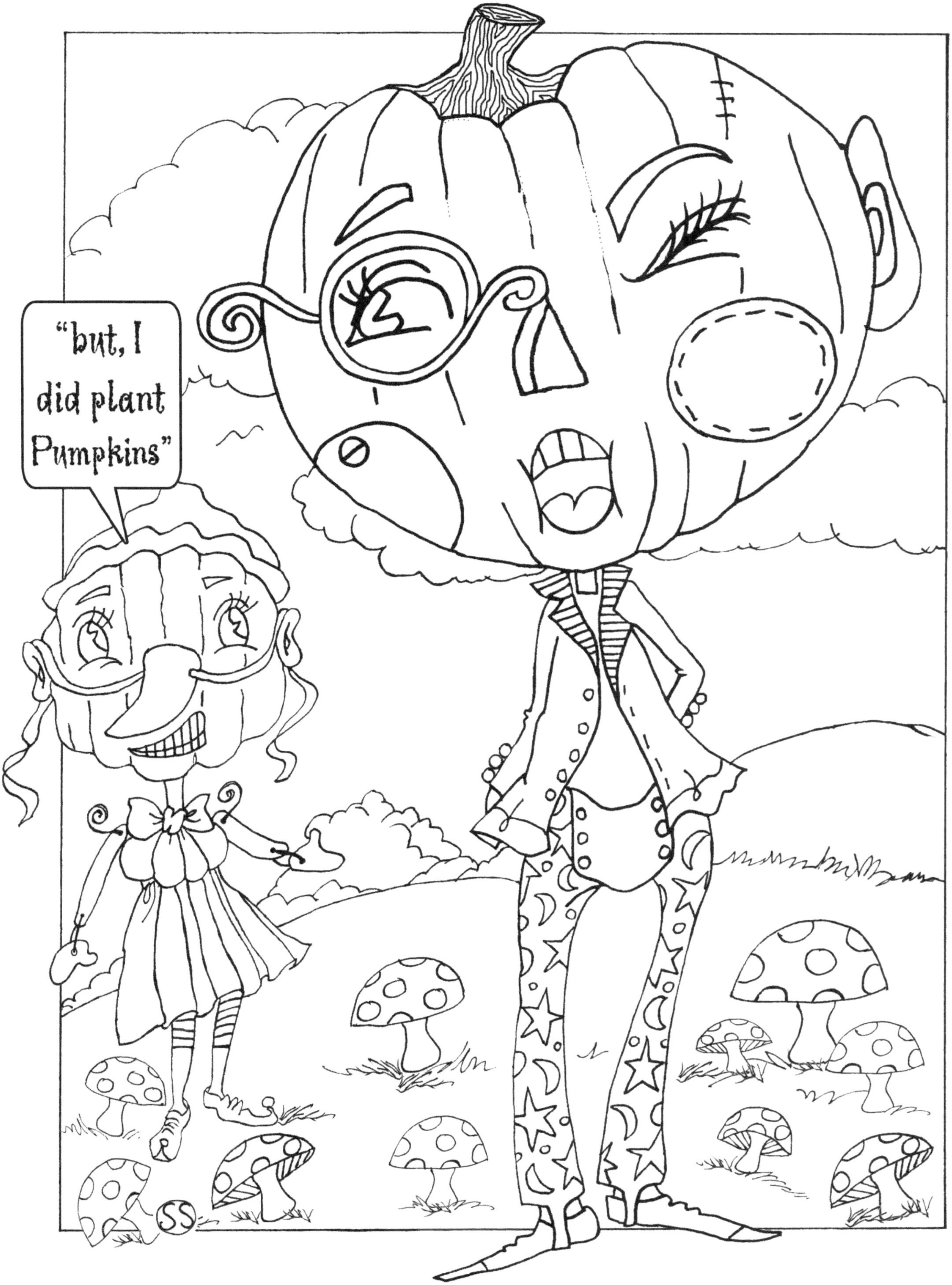
"but, I did plant Pumpkins"
SS

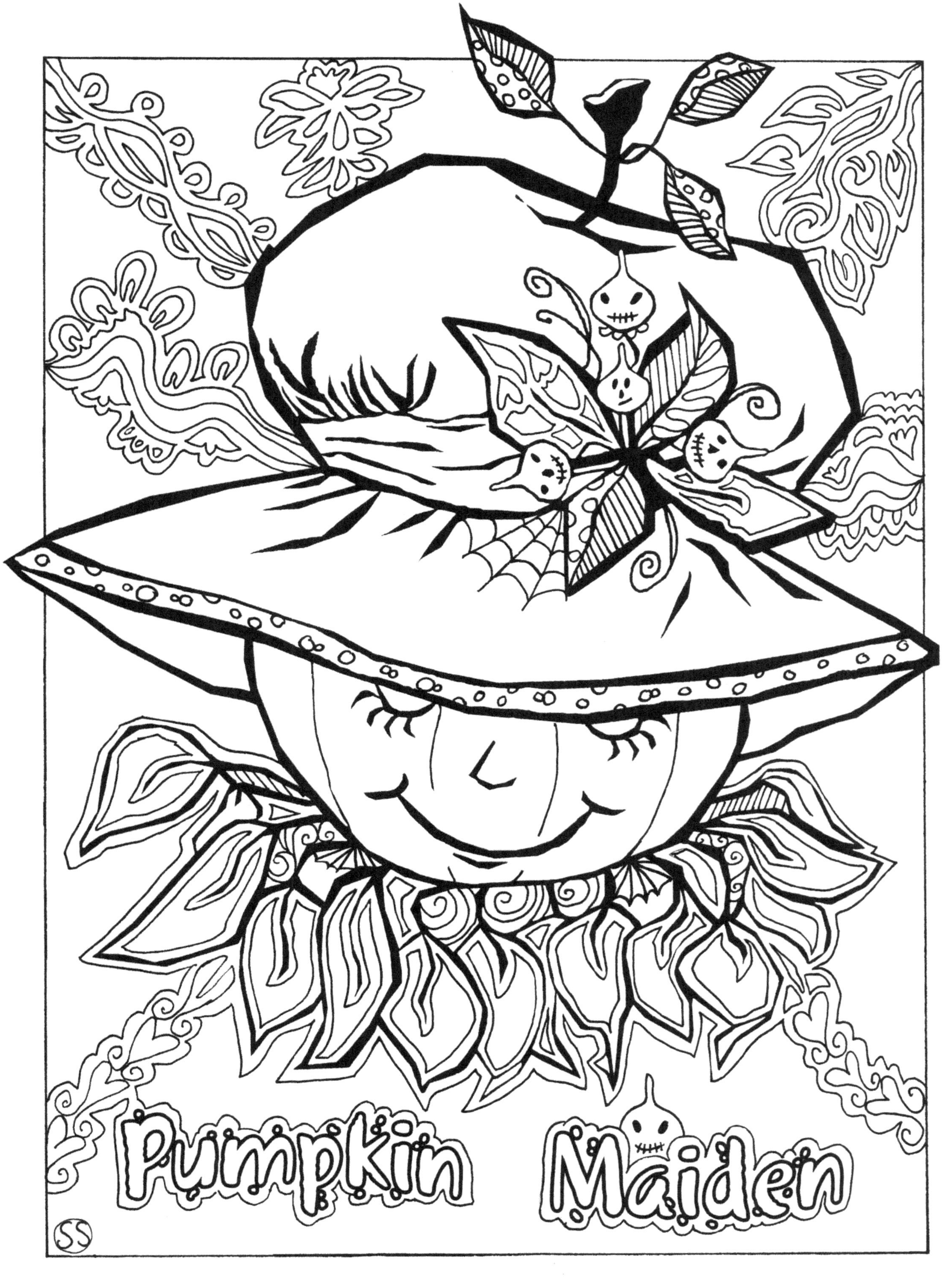
Pumpkin Maiden
SS

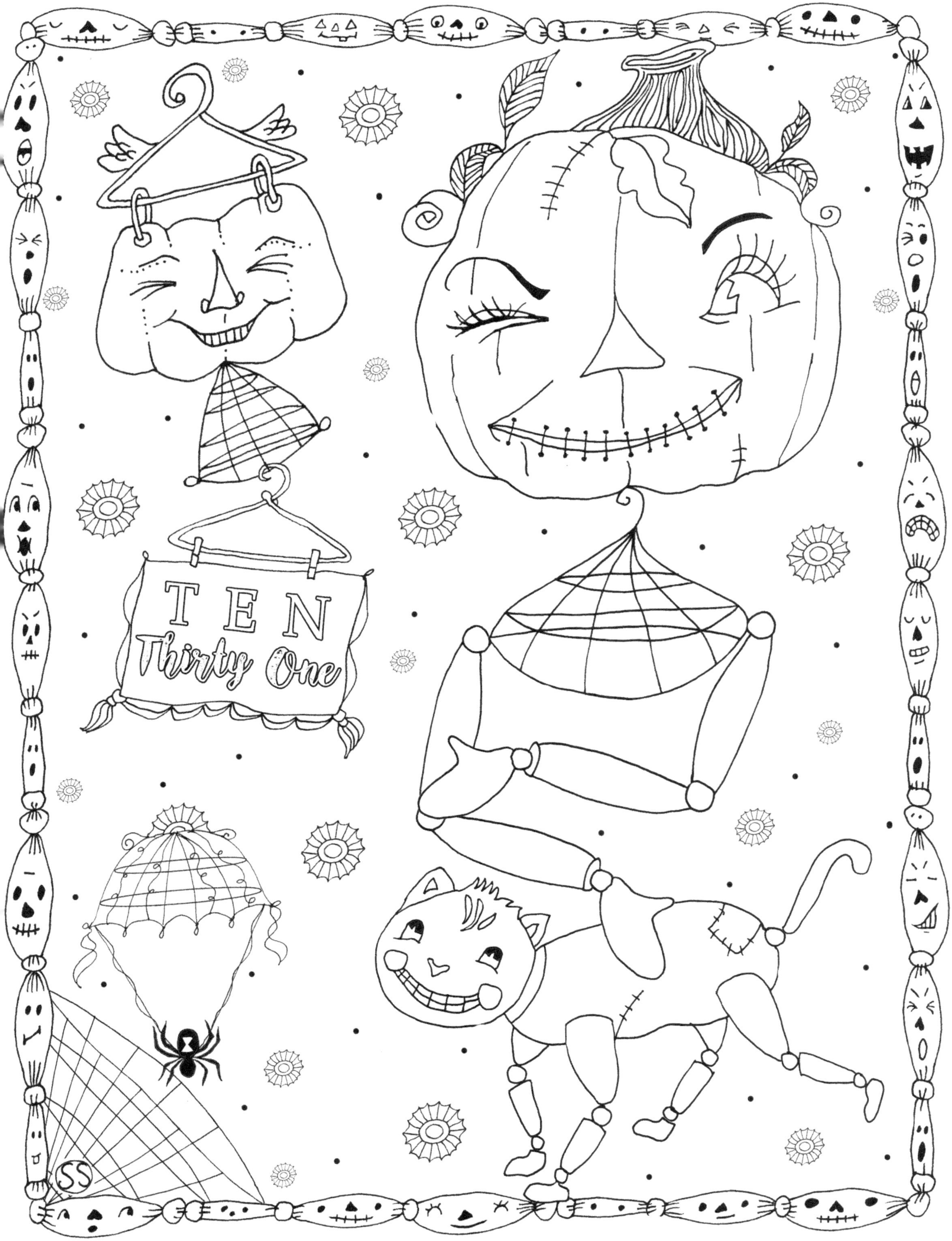
TEN
Thirty One
SS

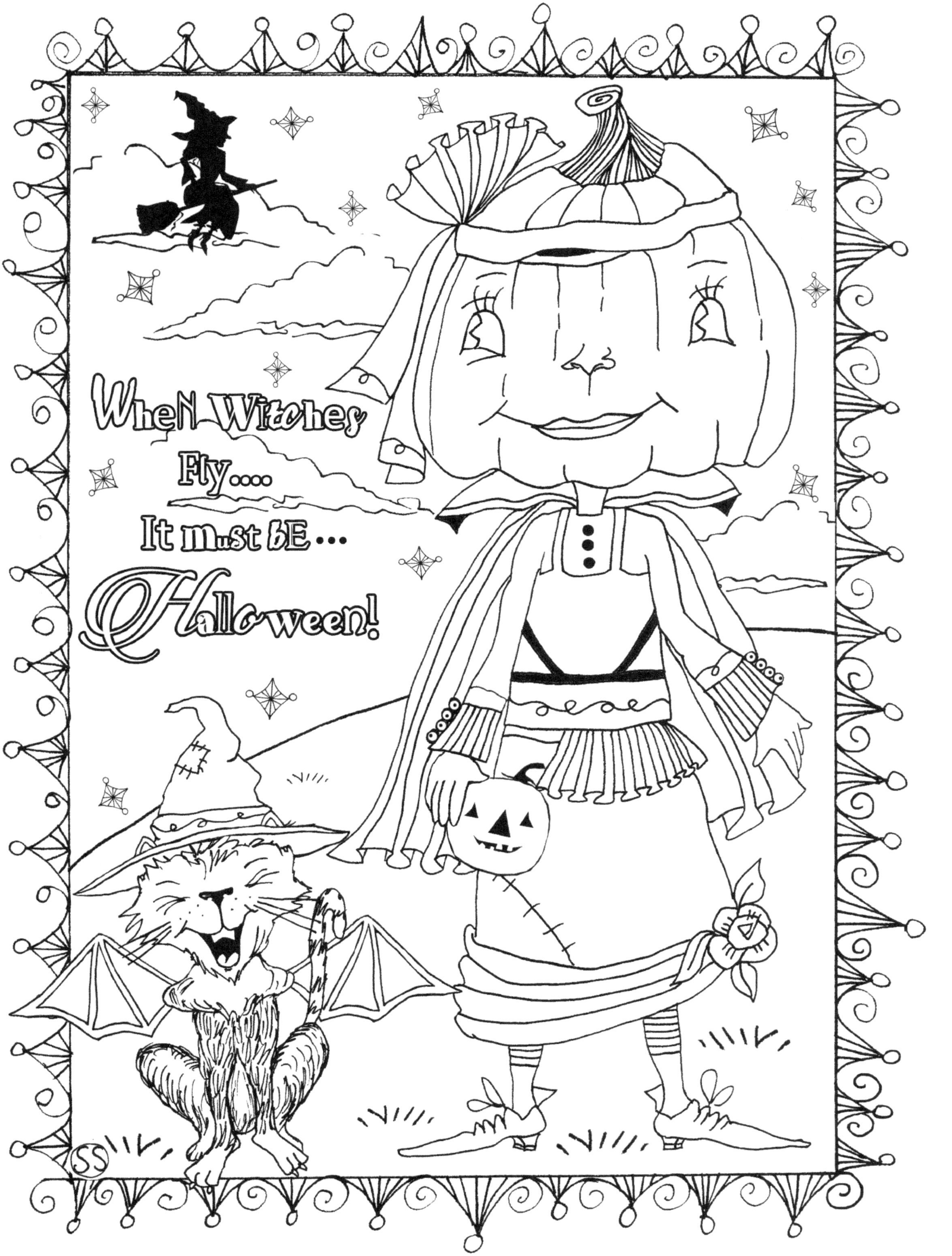
When Witches
Fly....
It must bE...
Halloween!
SS

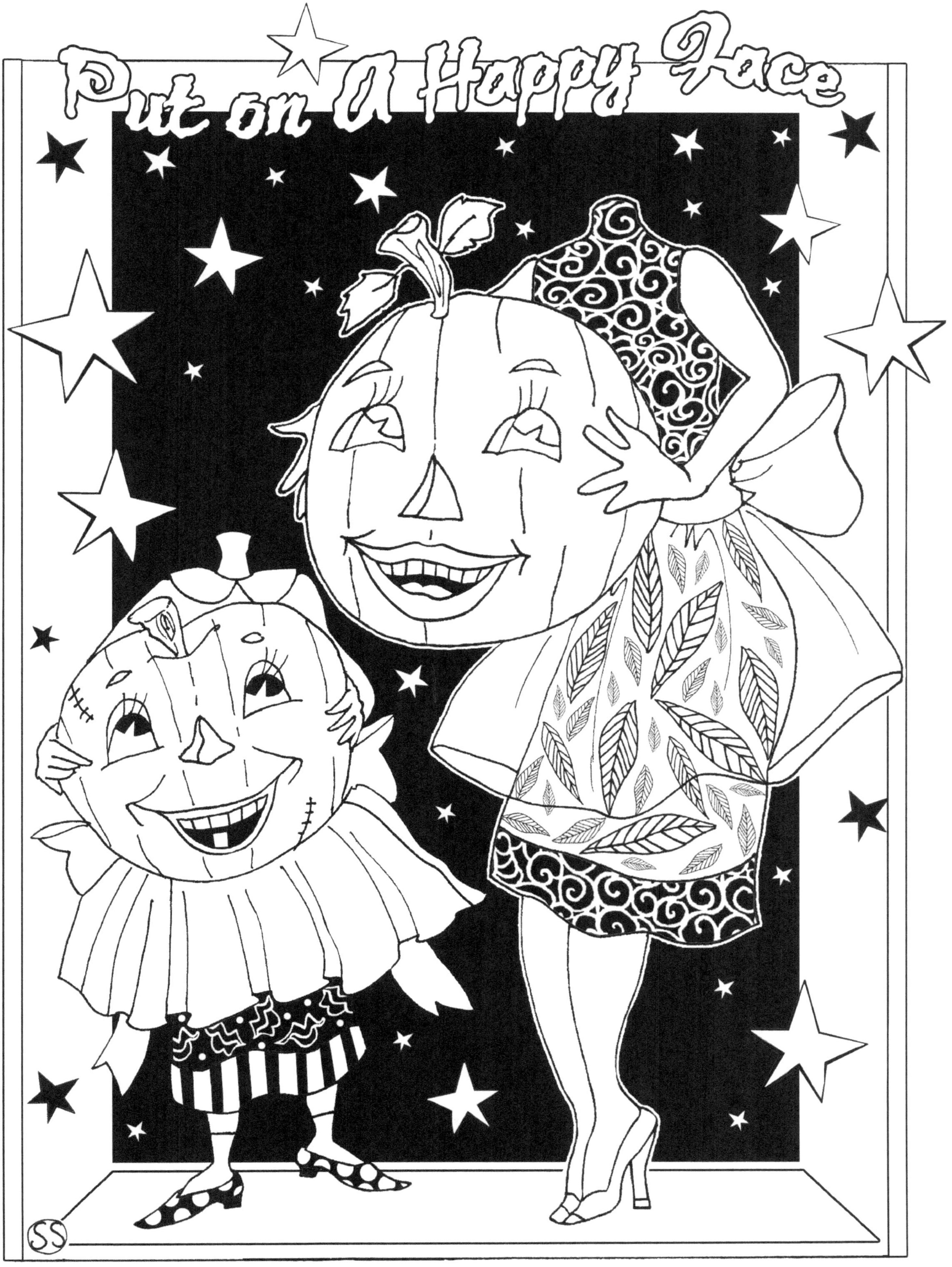
Put on A Happy Face
SS

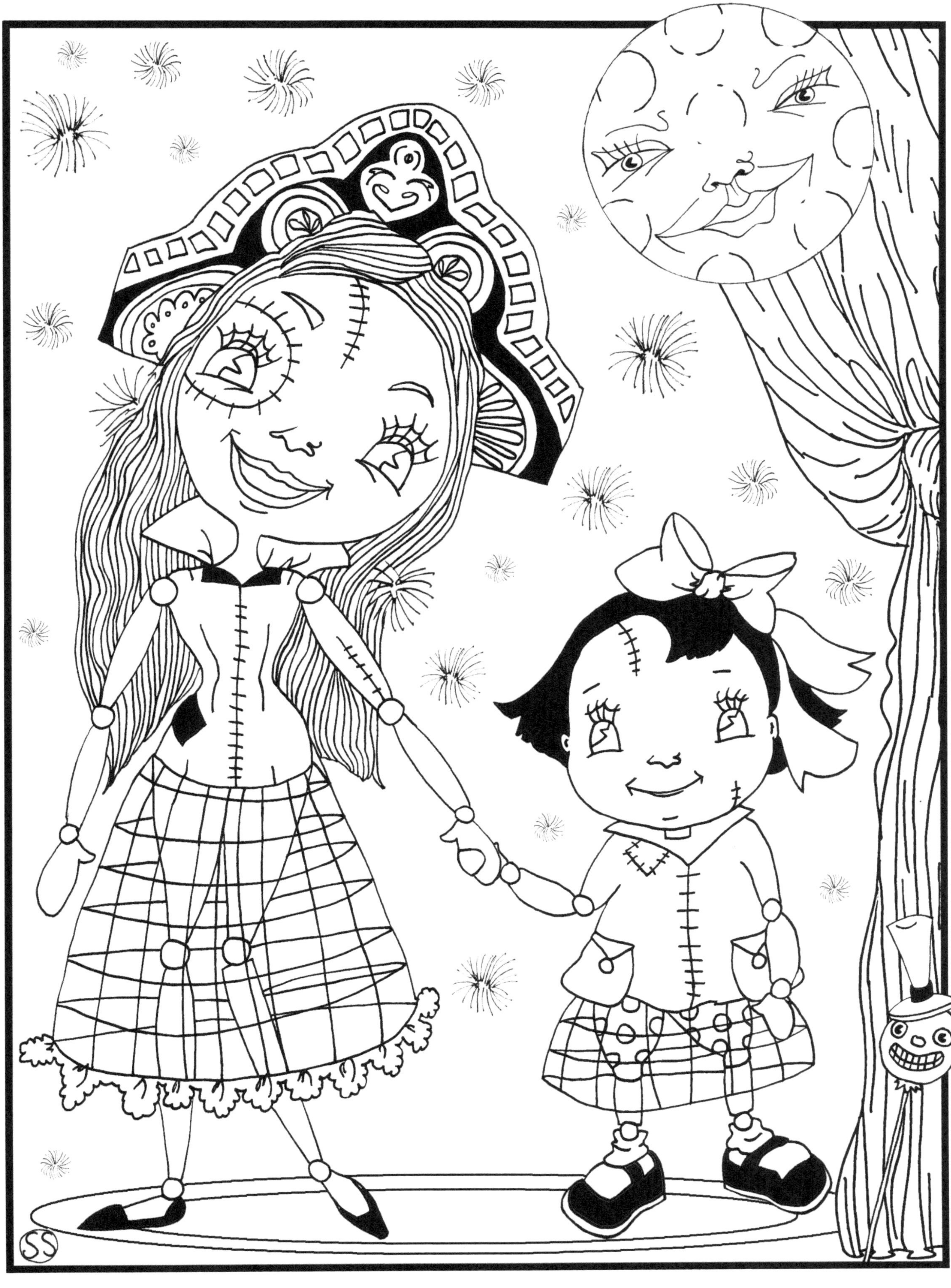
SS

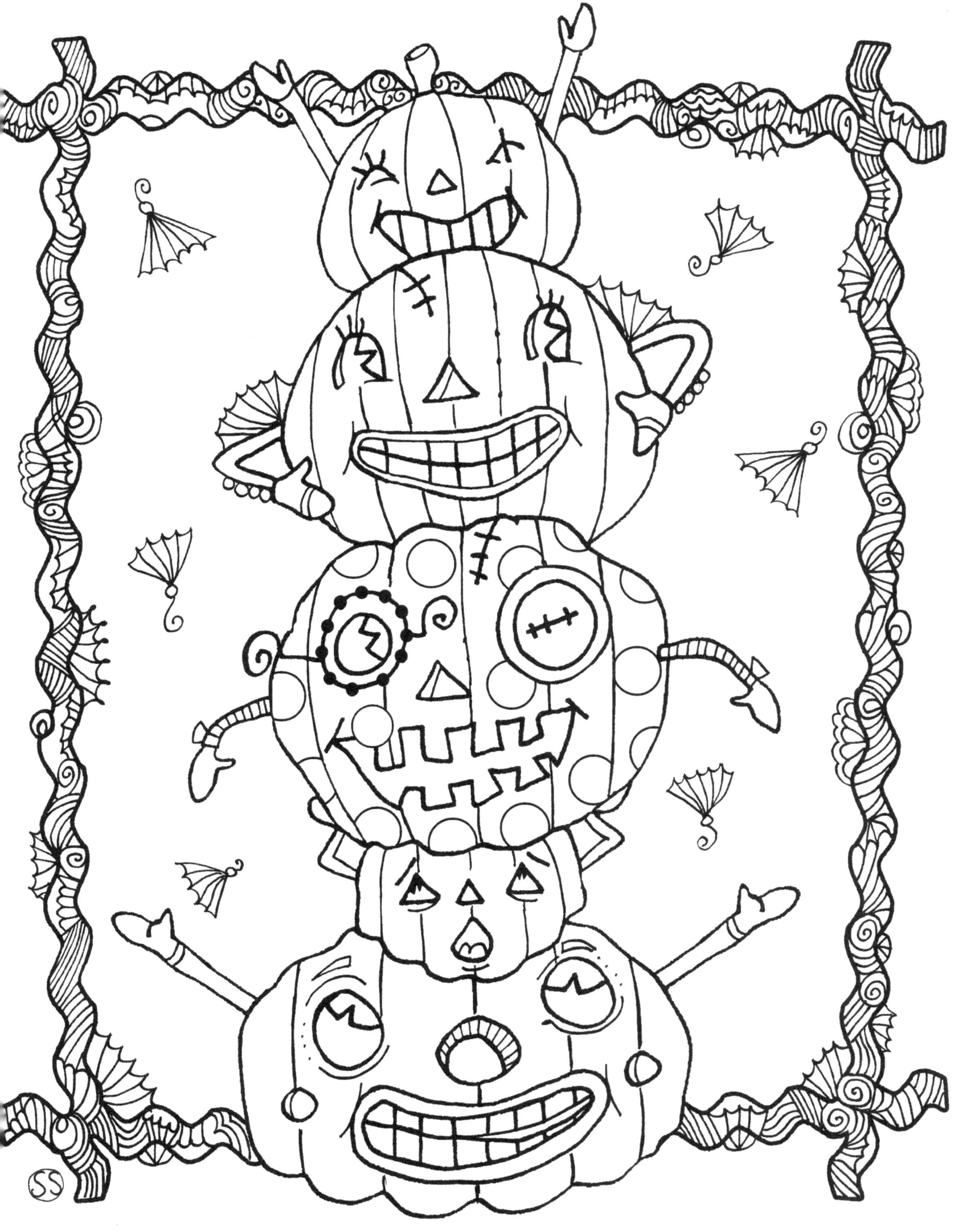

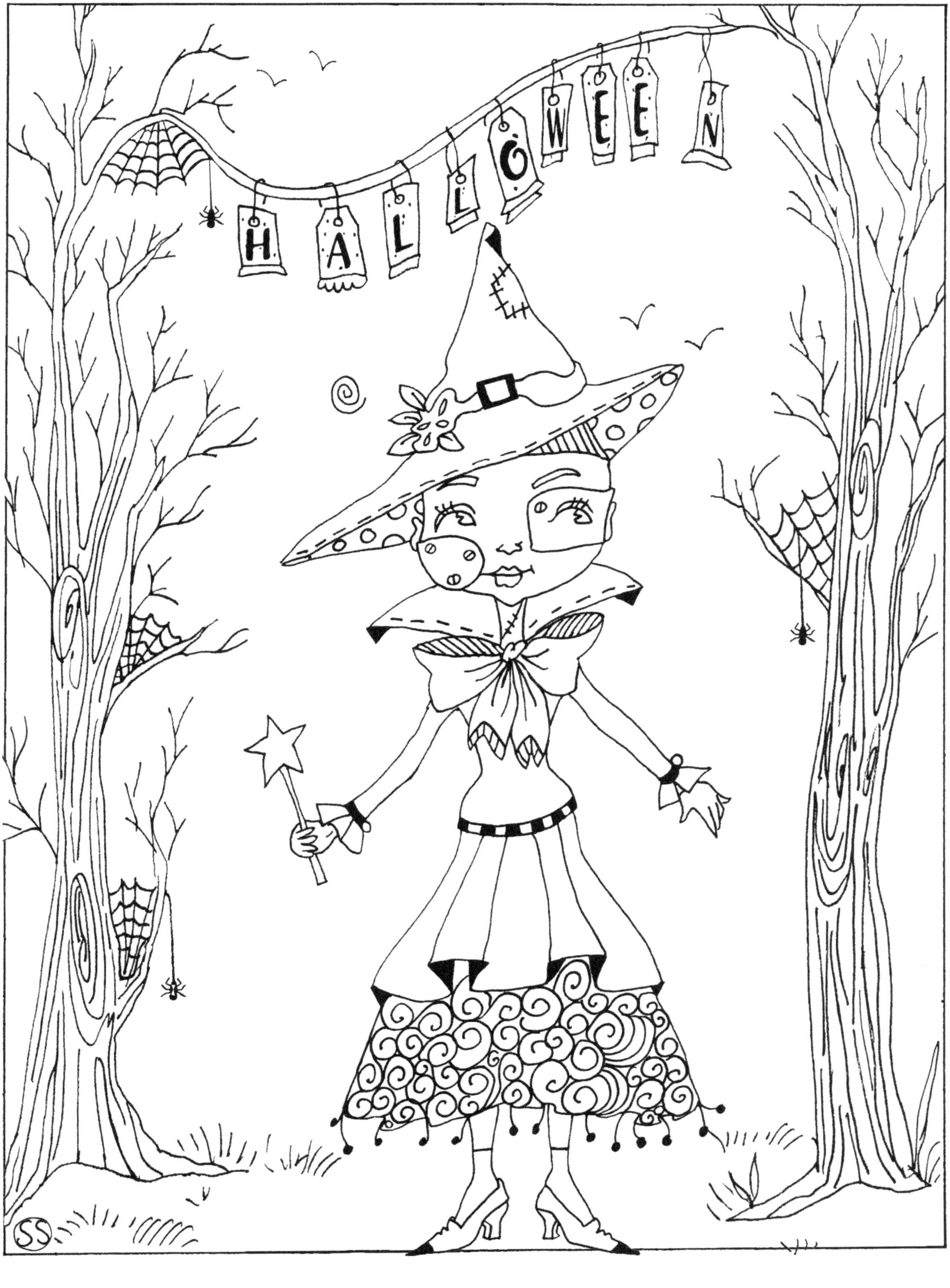
HALLOWEEN
SS

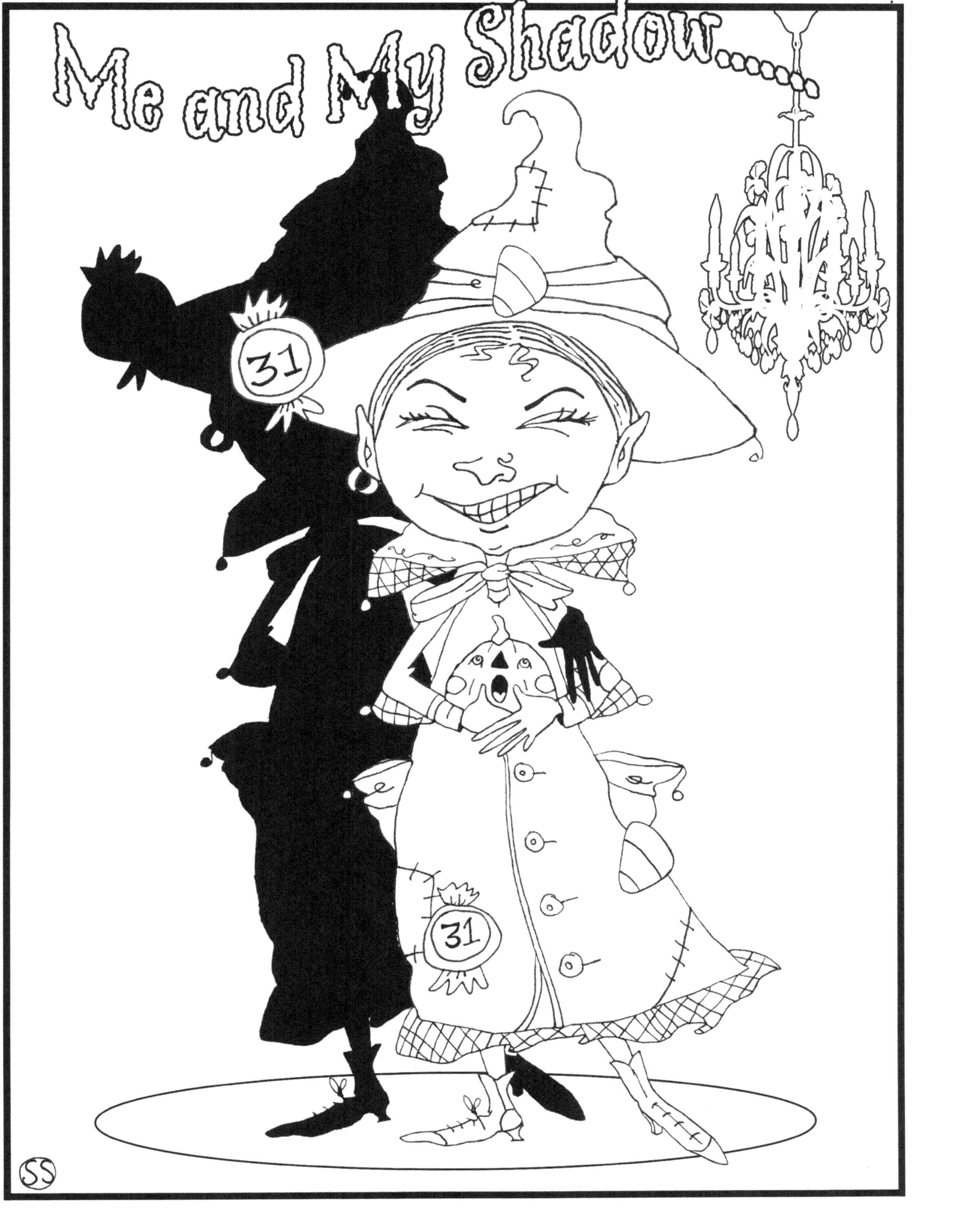
Me and My Shadow.......
31
31
SS

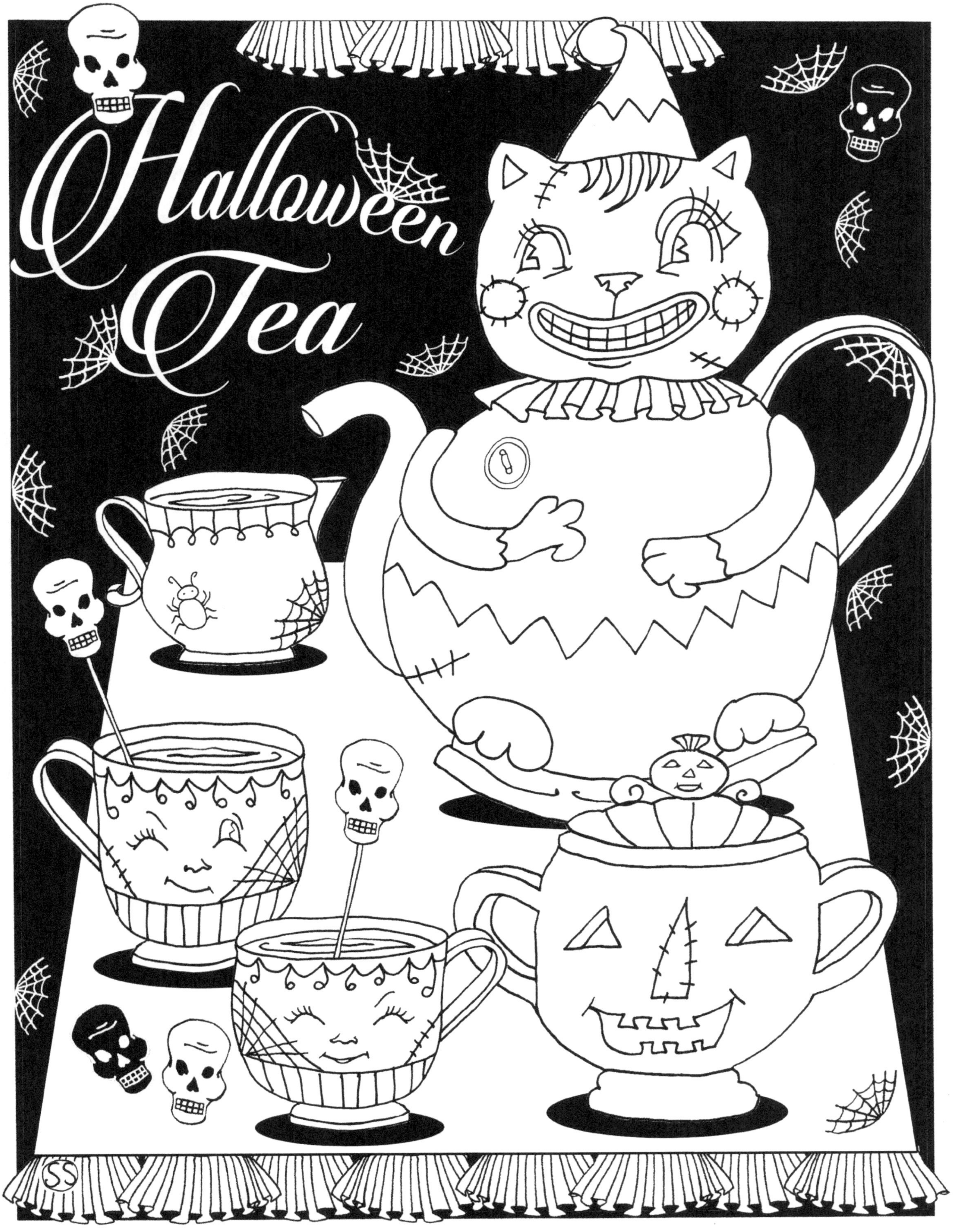
Halloween
Tea

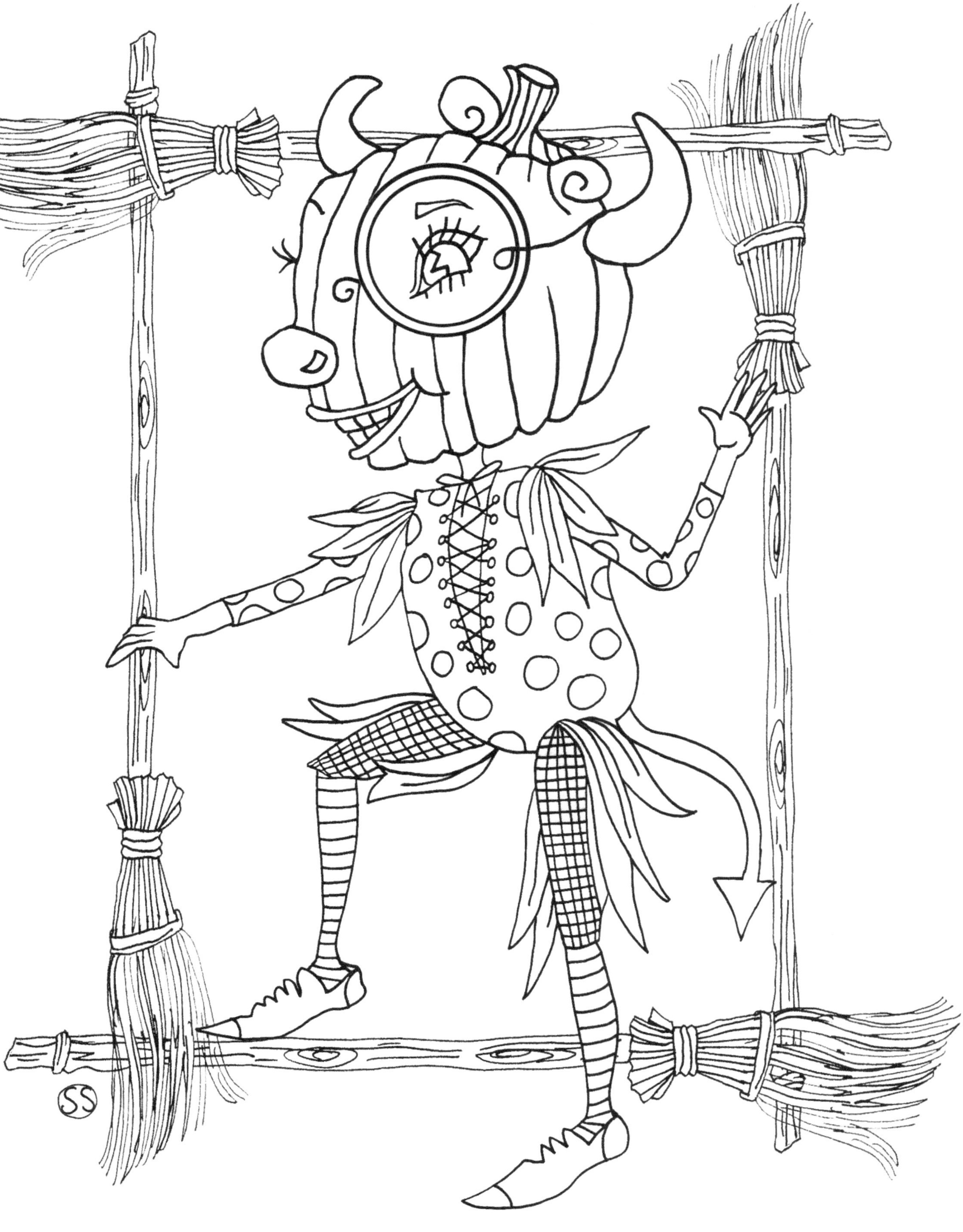
SS

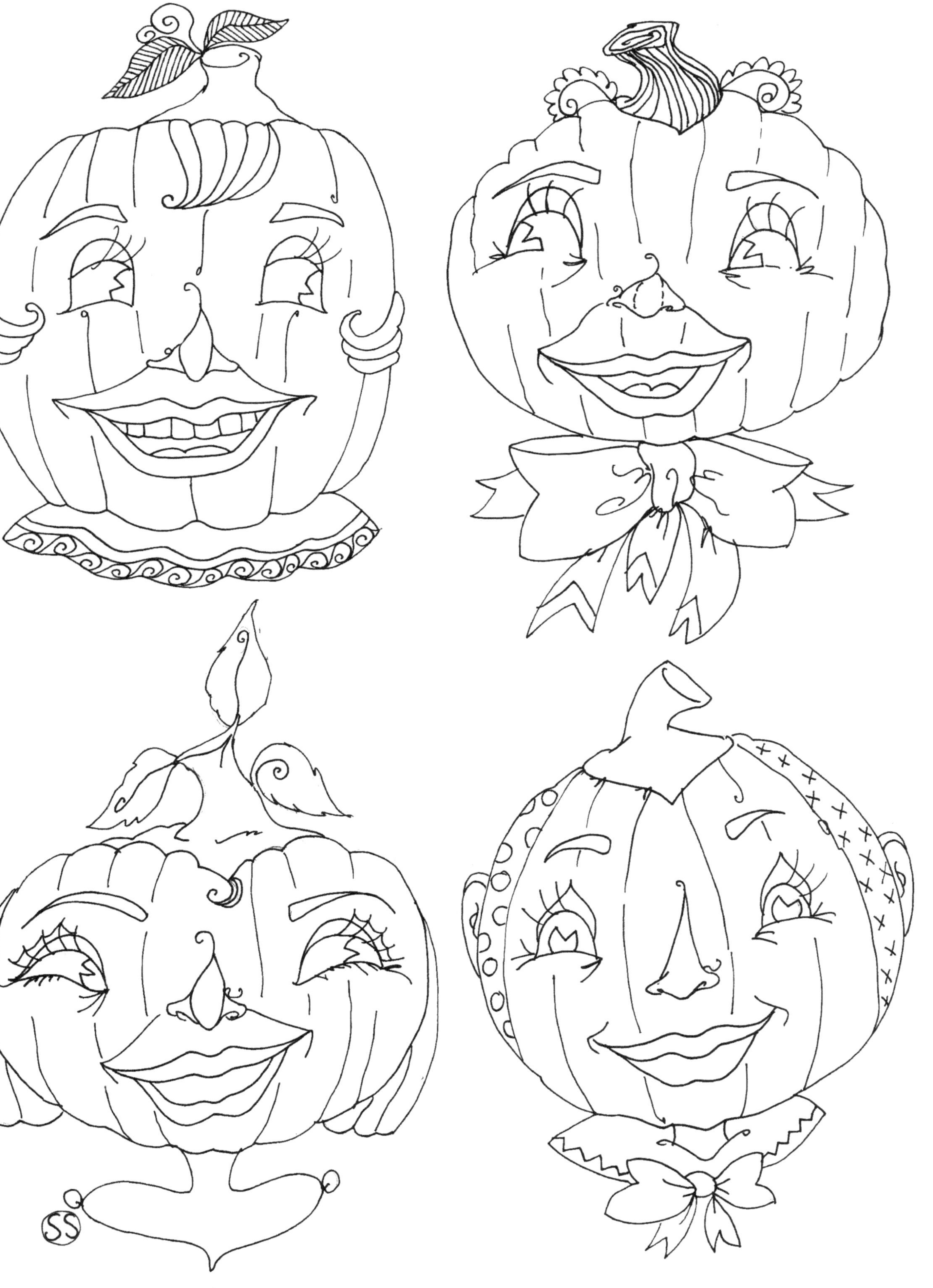

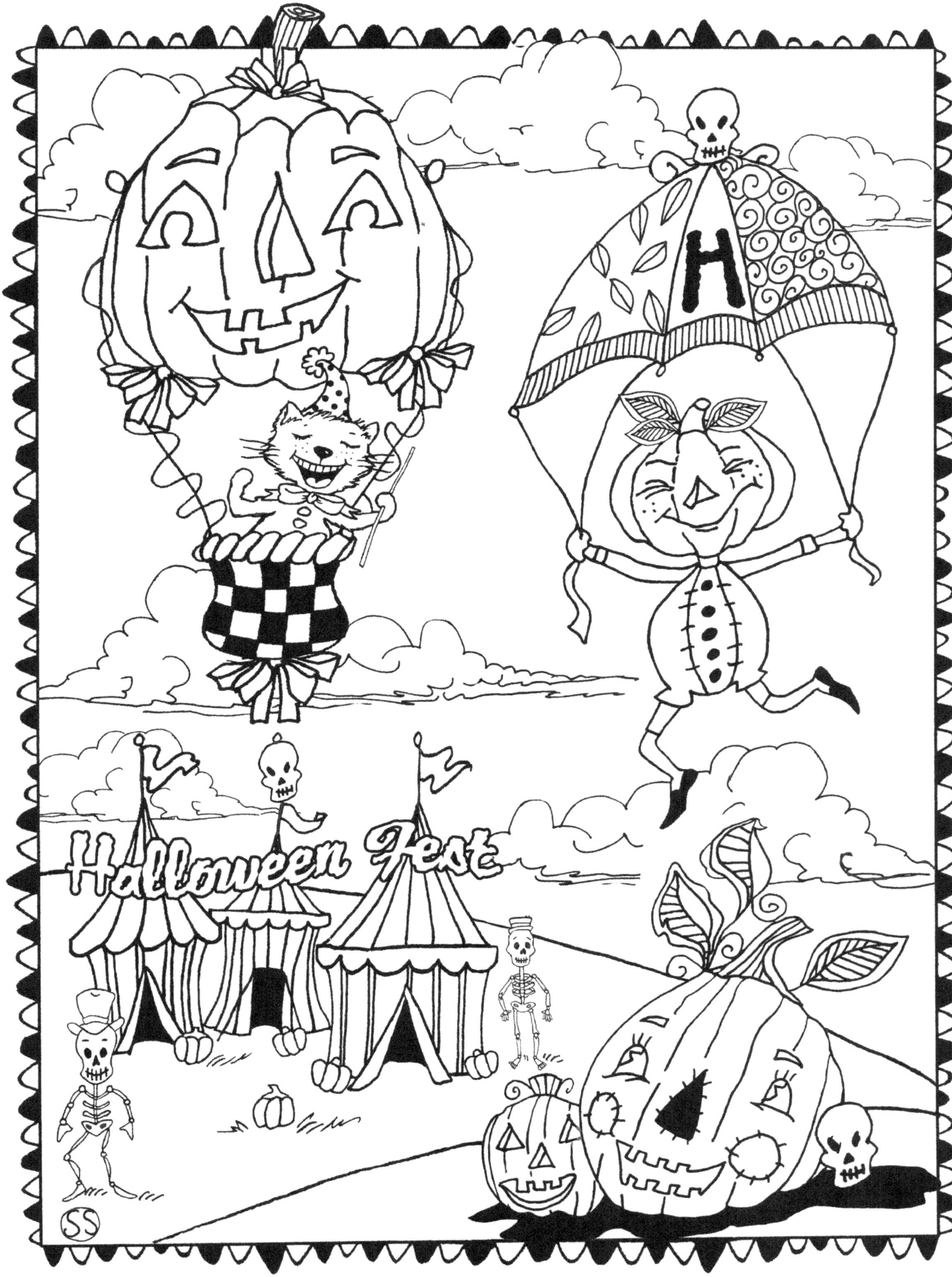
H
Halloween Fest
SS

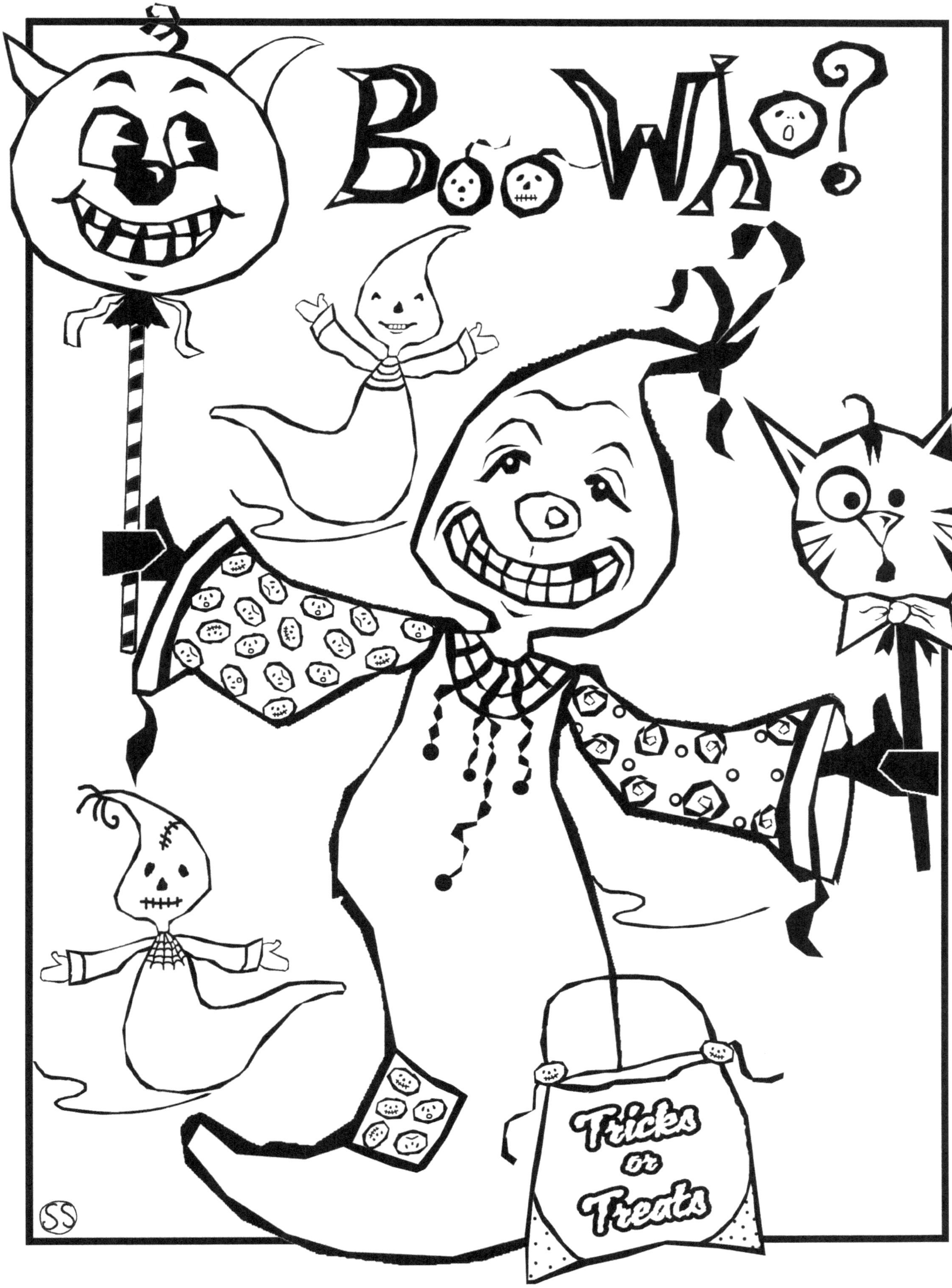
Boo Who?
Tricks or Treats
SS

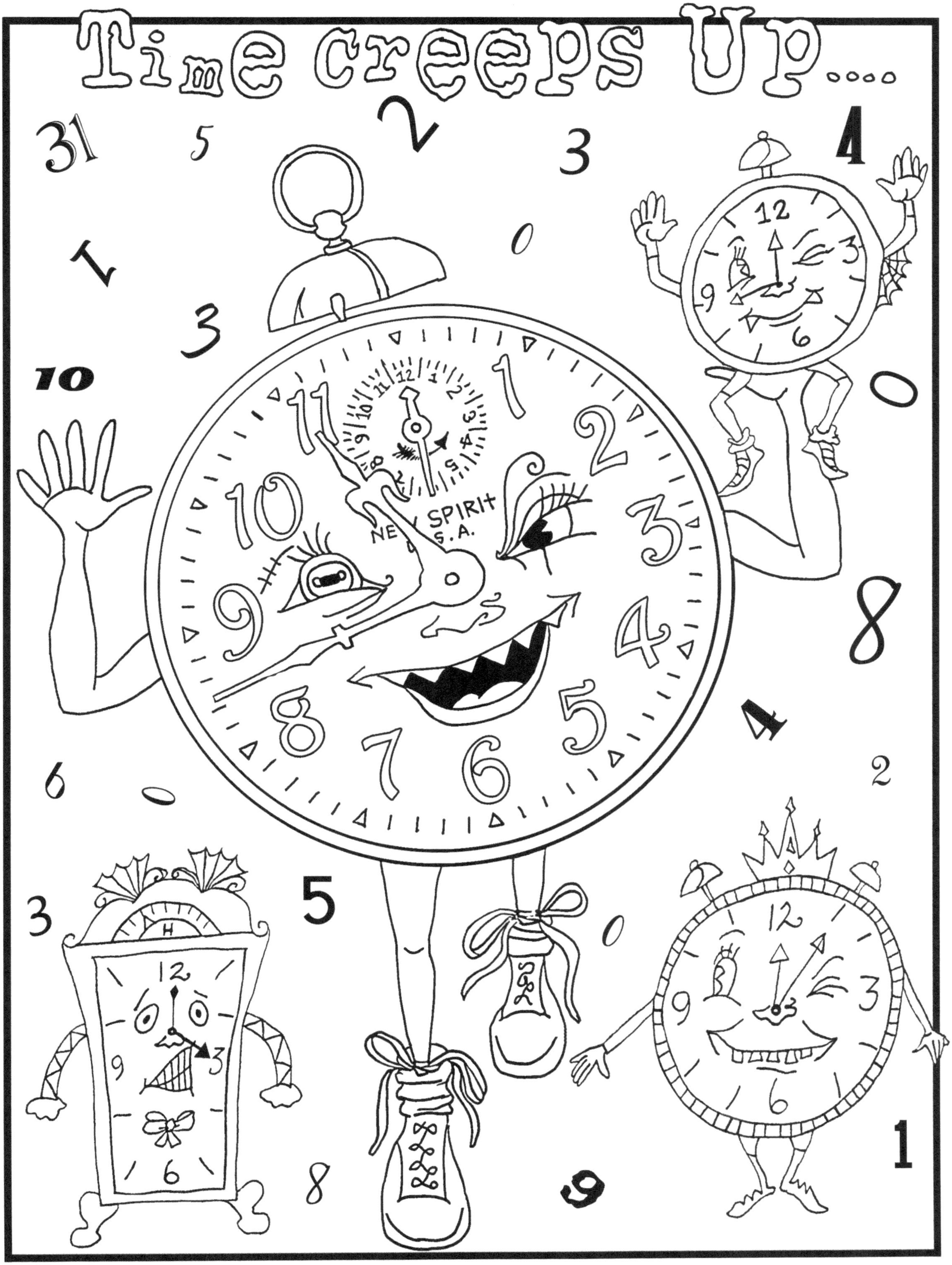
Time Creeps Up....
NEW SPIRIT

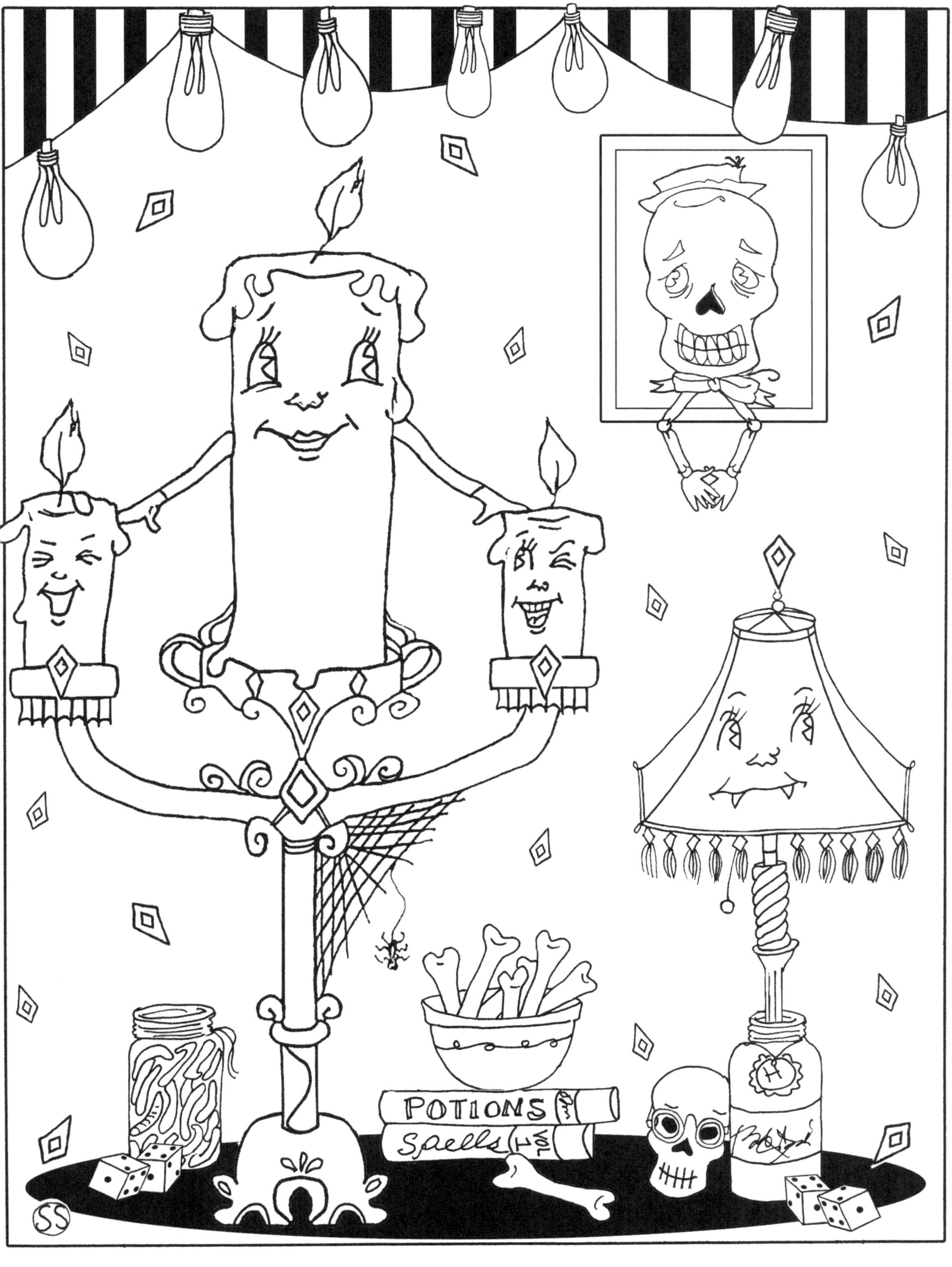
POTIONS
Spells